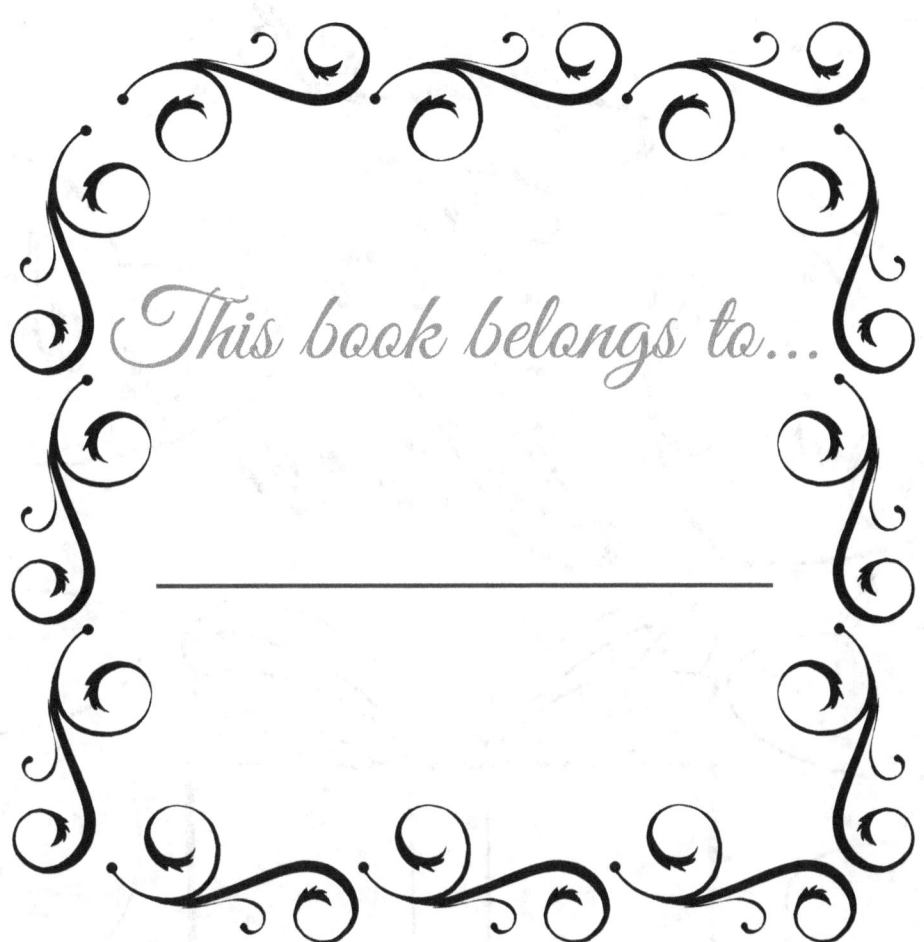

This book belongs to...

_____

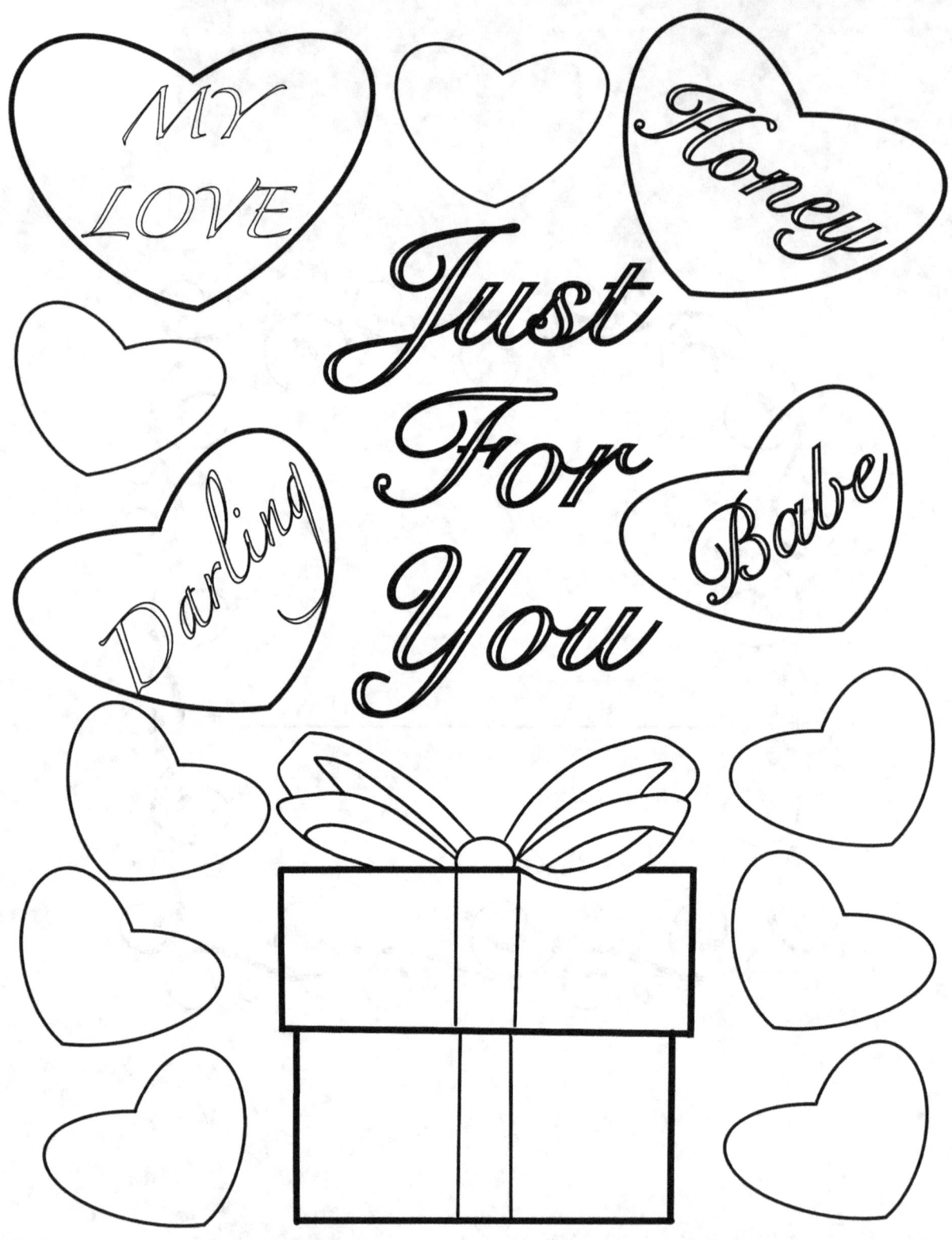

Copyright 2020 Ron Yarosh Books

No portion of this book may be reproduced or copied by any means including electronic or mechanical without the express permission of the author.

Dear colorist friend,

Thank you very much for purchasing my latest original Adult Coloring Book. I hope you enjoy adding your colorful creative touch to the images in this newest edition called, **ROMANCE AND RELAXATION**.

I'm sure you will find it romantic, relaxing…and heart warming.

As Ralph Waldo Emerson said, "Every artist was once an amateur."

More of my unique adult coloring books are in the process of being created and published. Look for them on Amazon and other publishing platforms

If you like this book, please give me a review, and tell your colorist friends about it.

Now, let the romance and relaxation begin. Get out your favorite colors and go to town.

Your friend,

Art King

REMEMBER TO PLACE A SHEET OF PAPER BETWEEN YOUR COLORING PAGES TO AVOID THE POSSIBILITY OF BLEED THROUGH TO THE FOLLOWING PAGE.

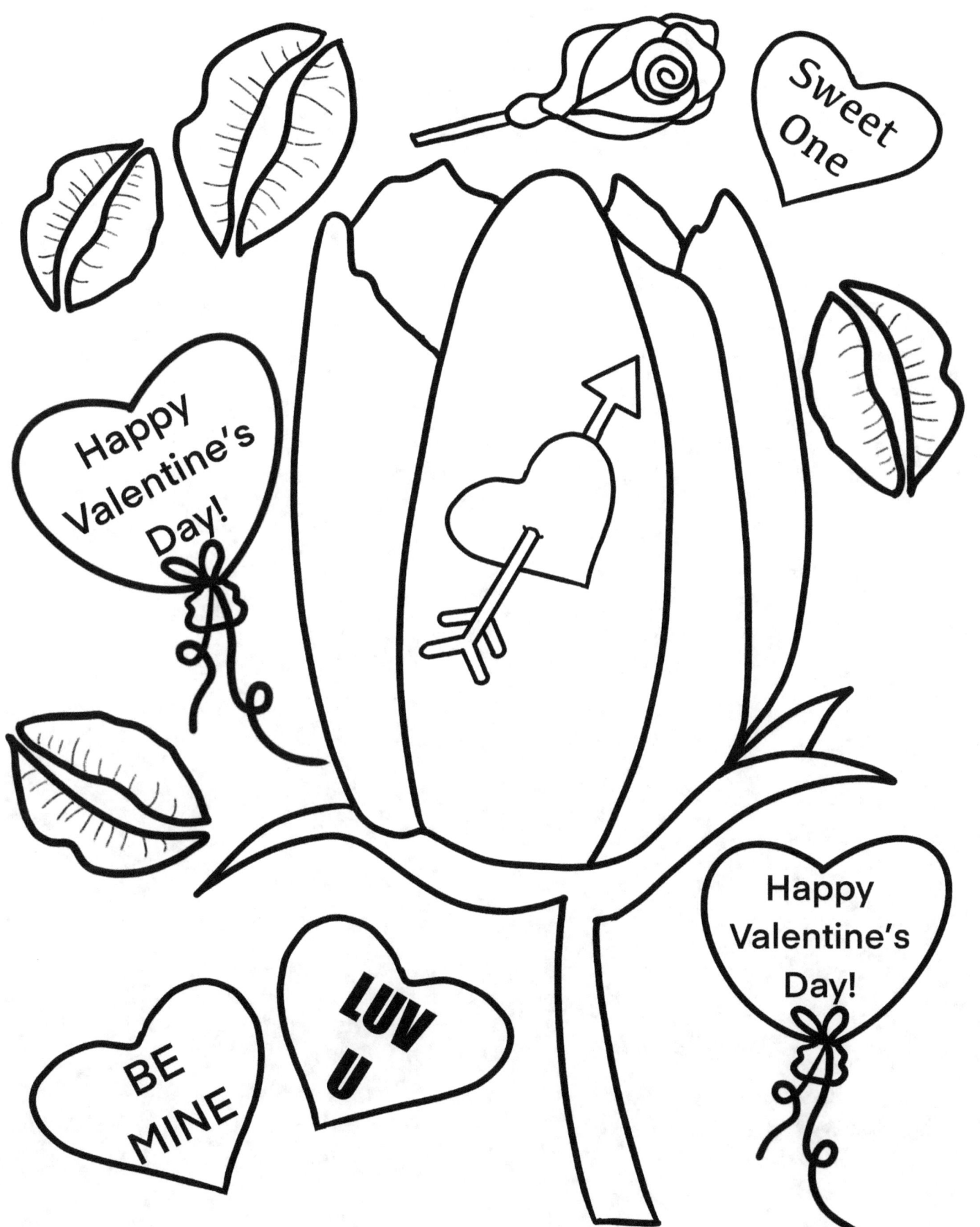

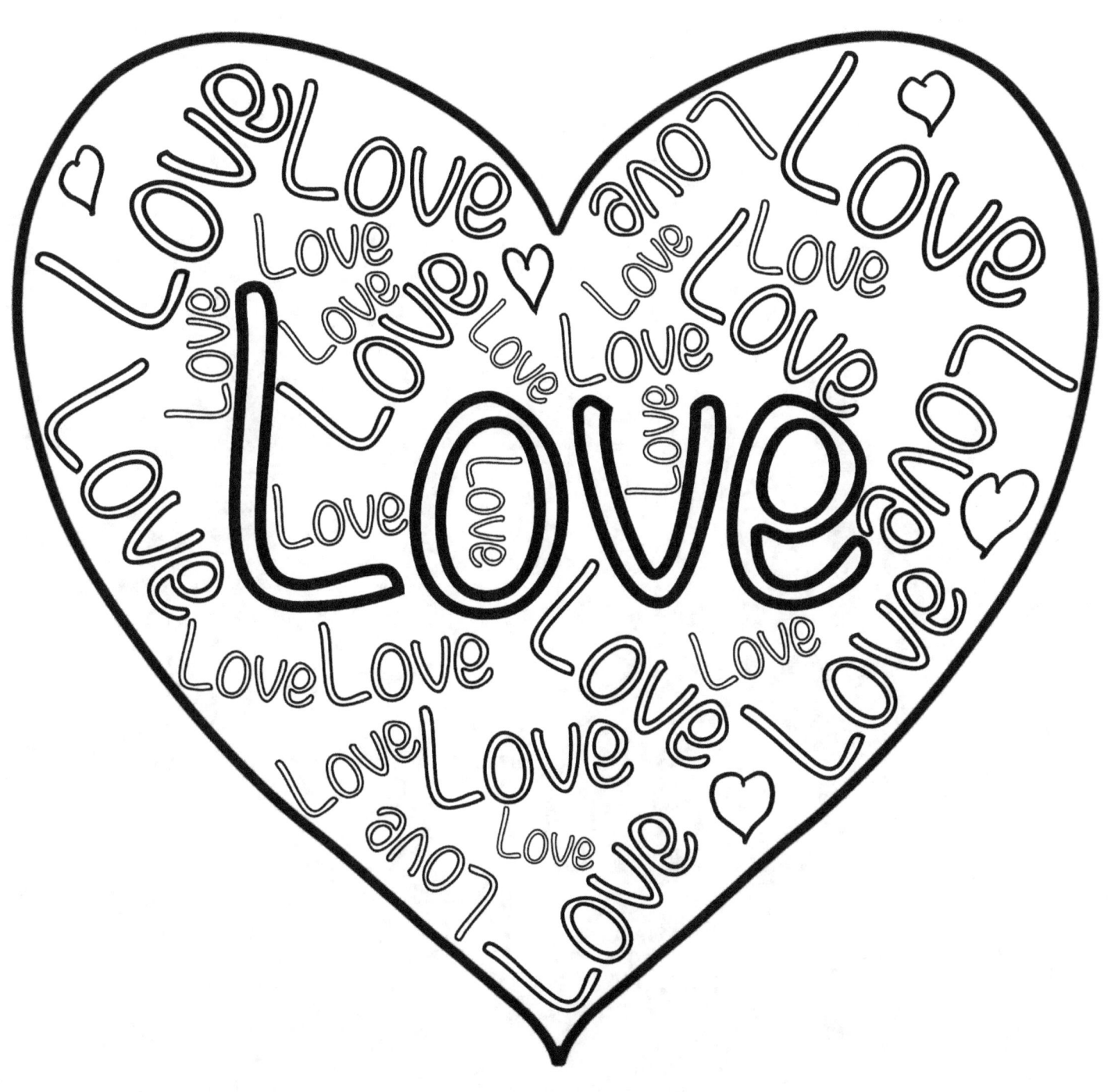

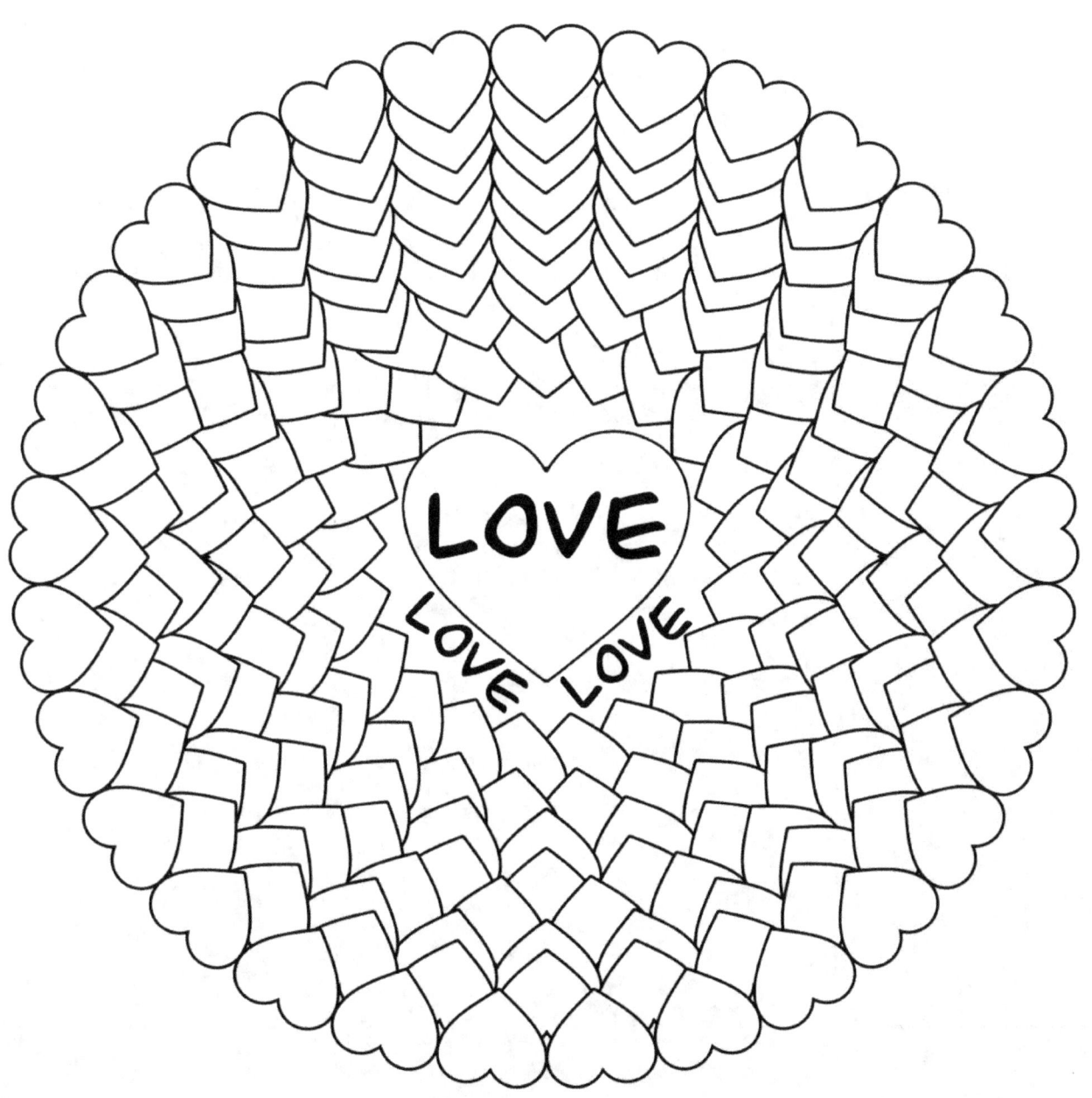

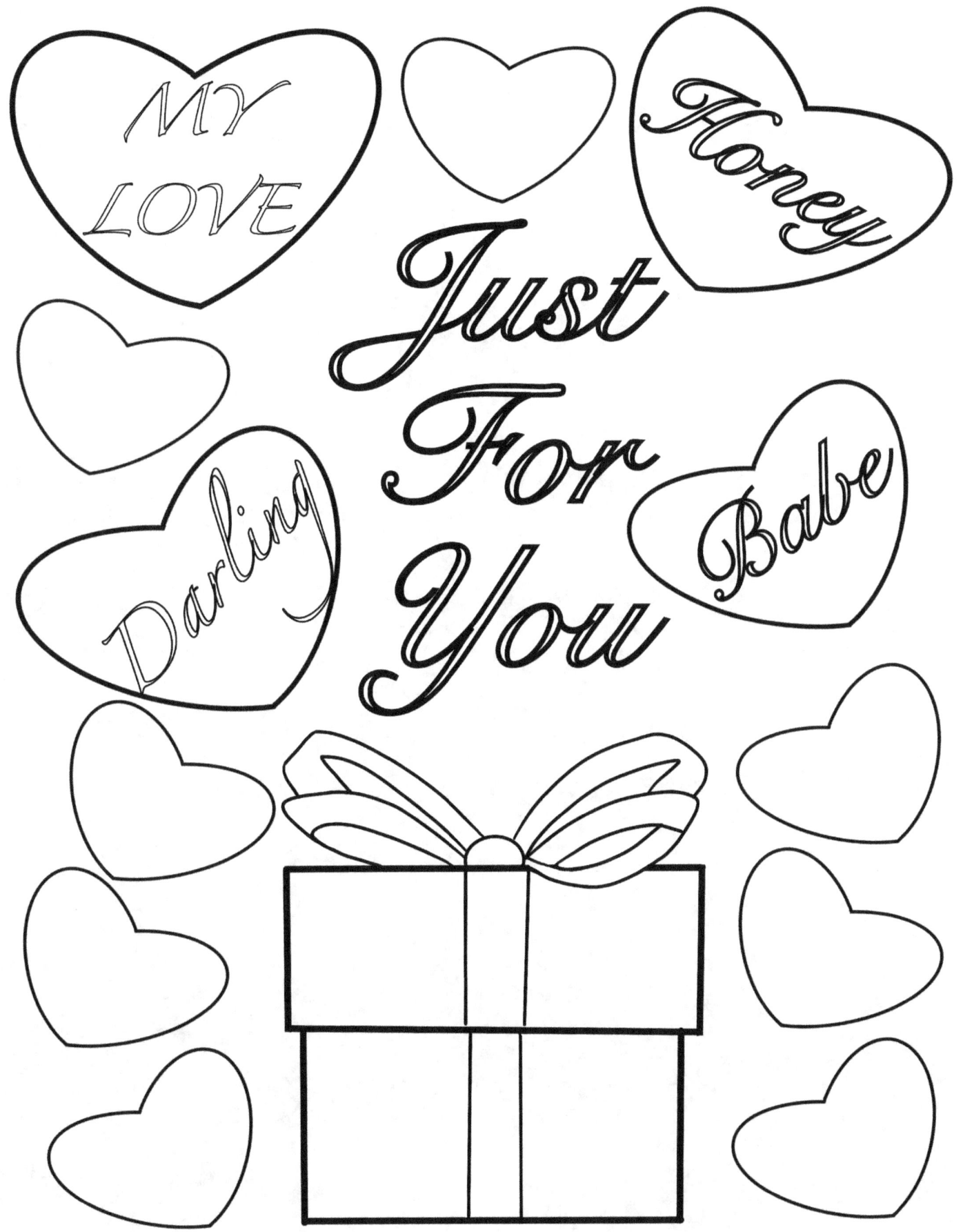

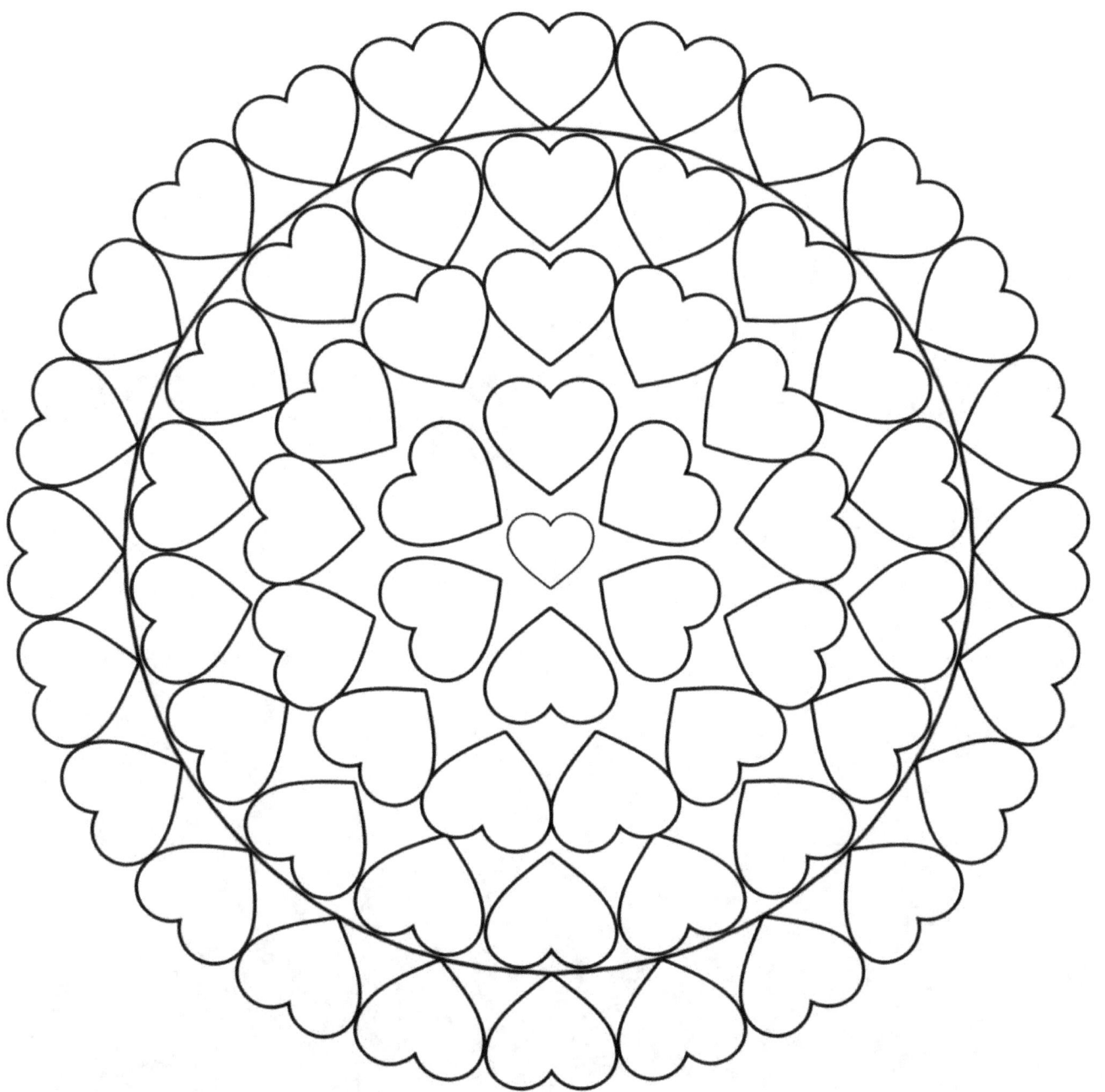

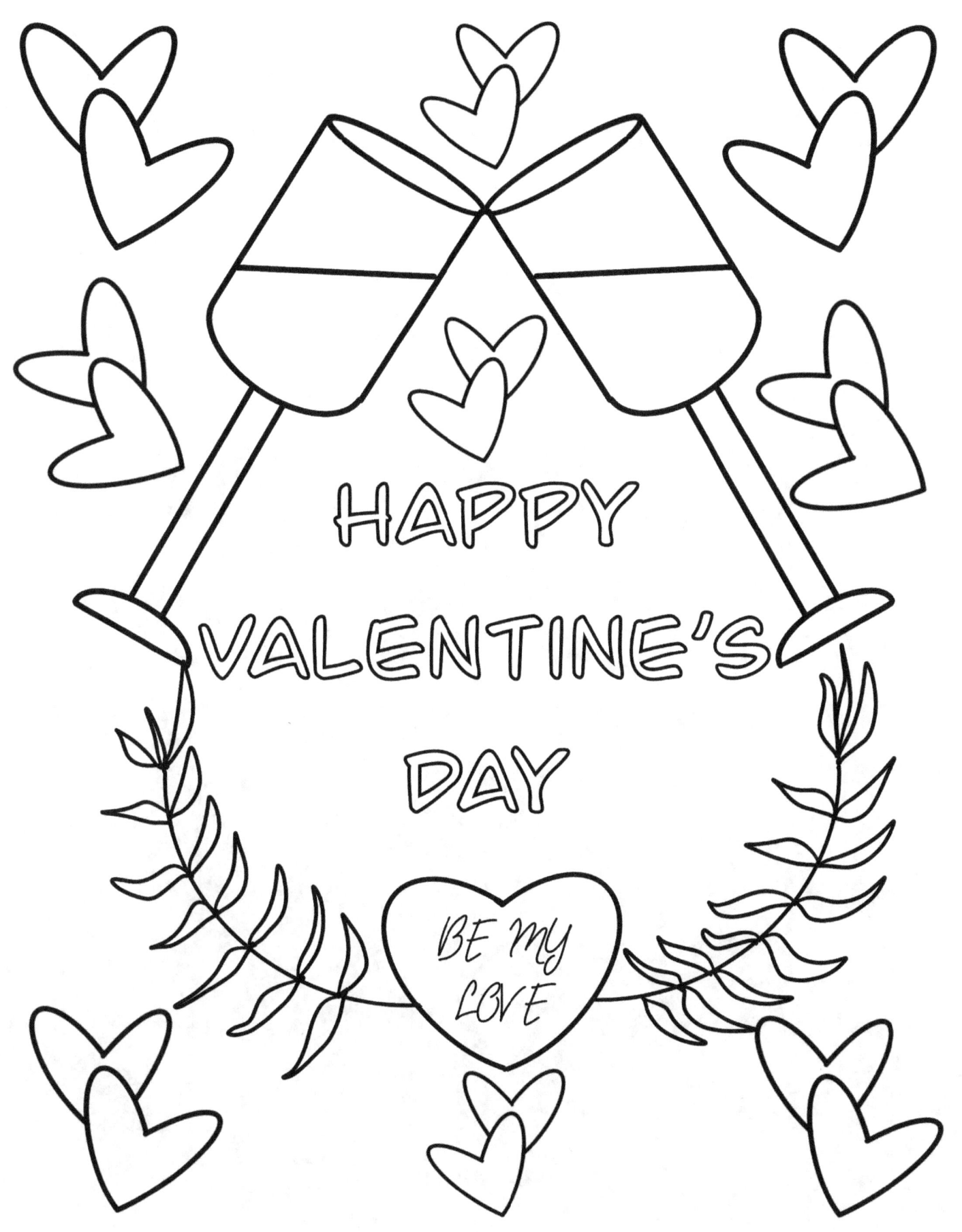

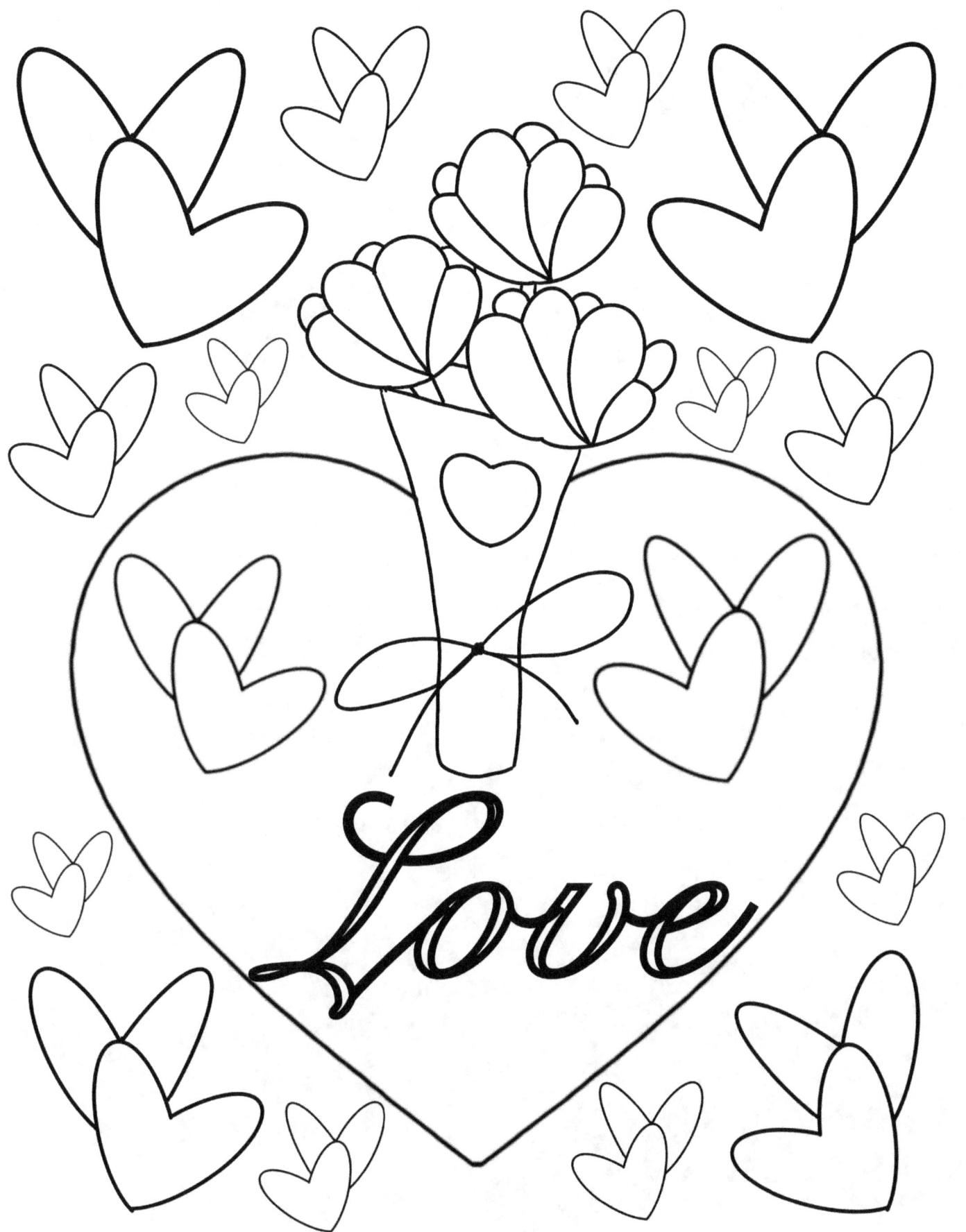

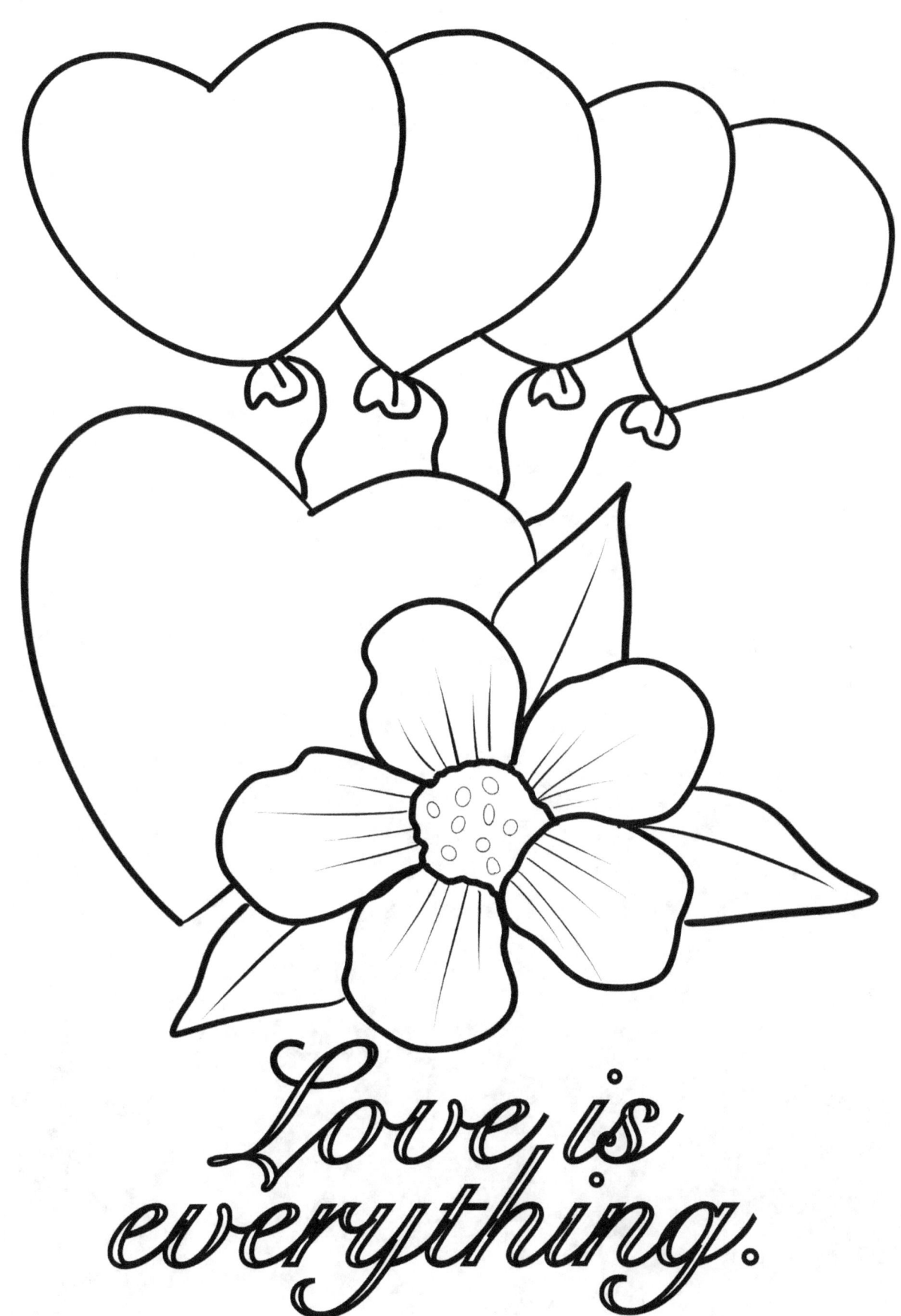

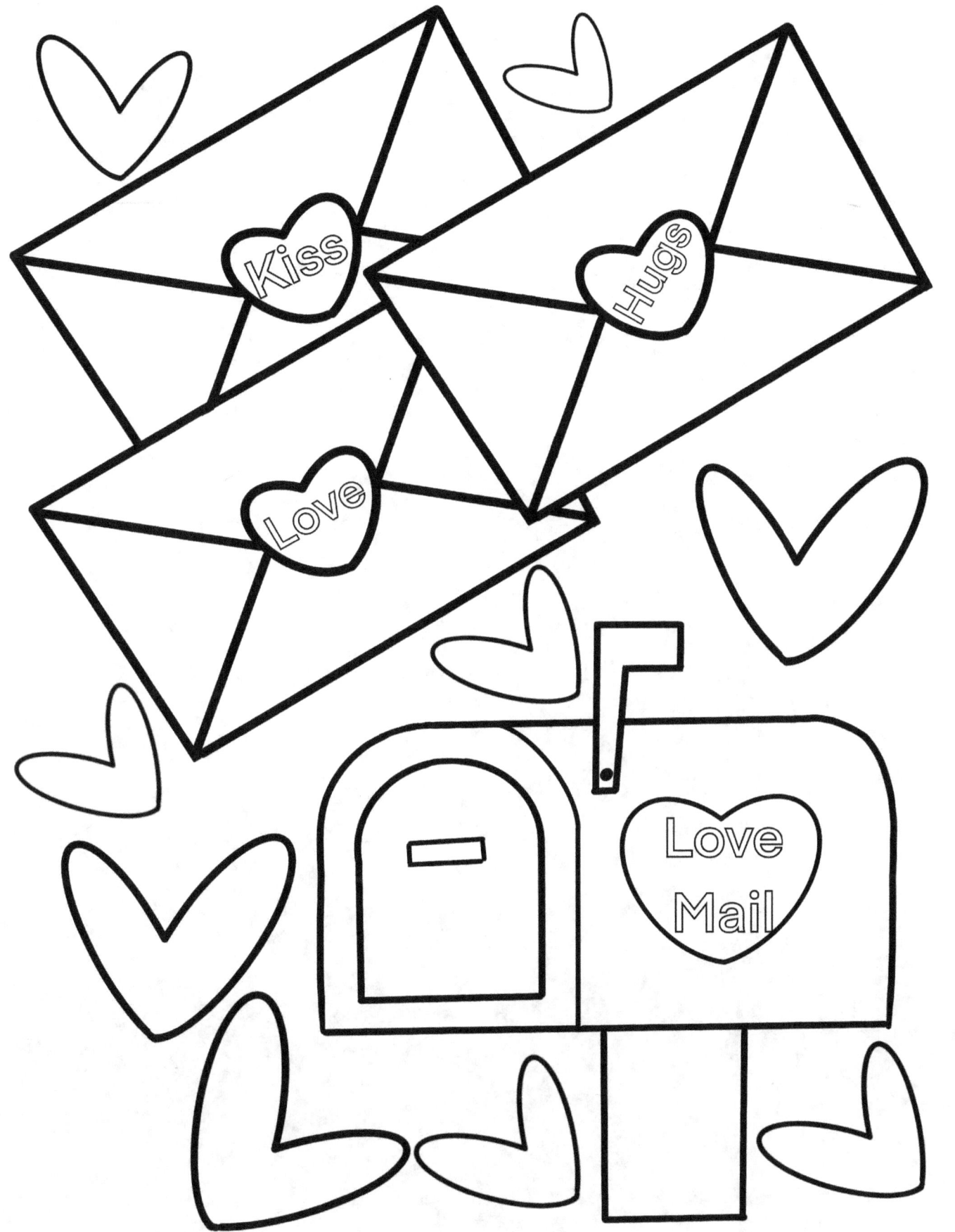

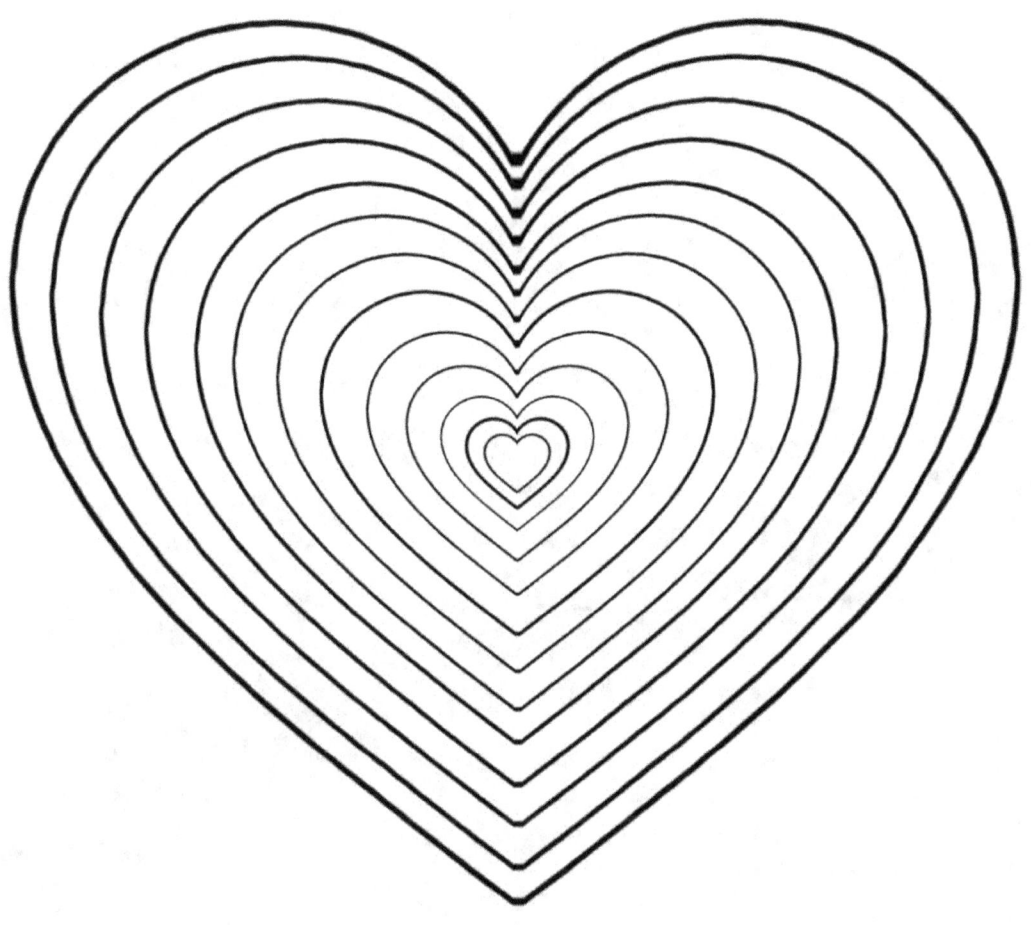

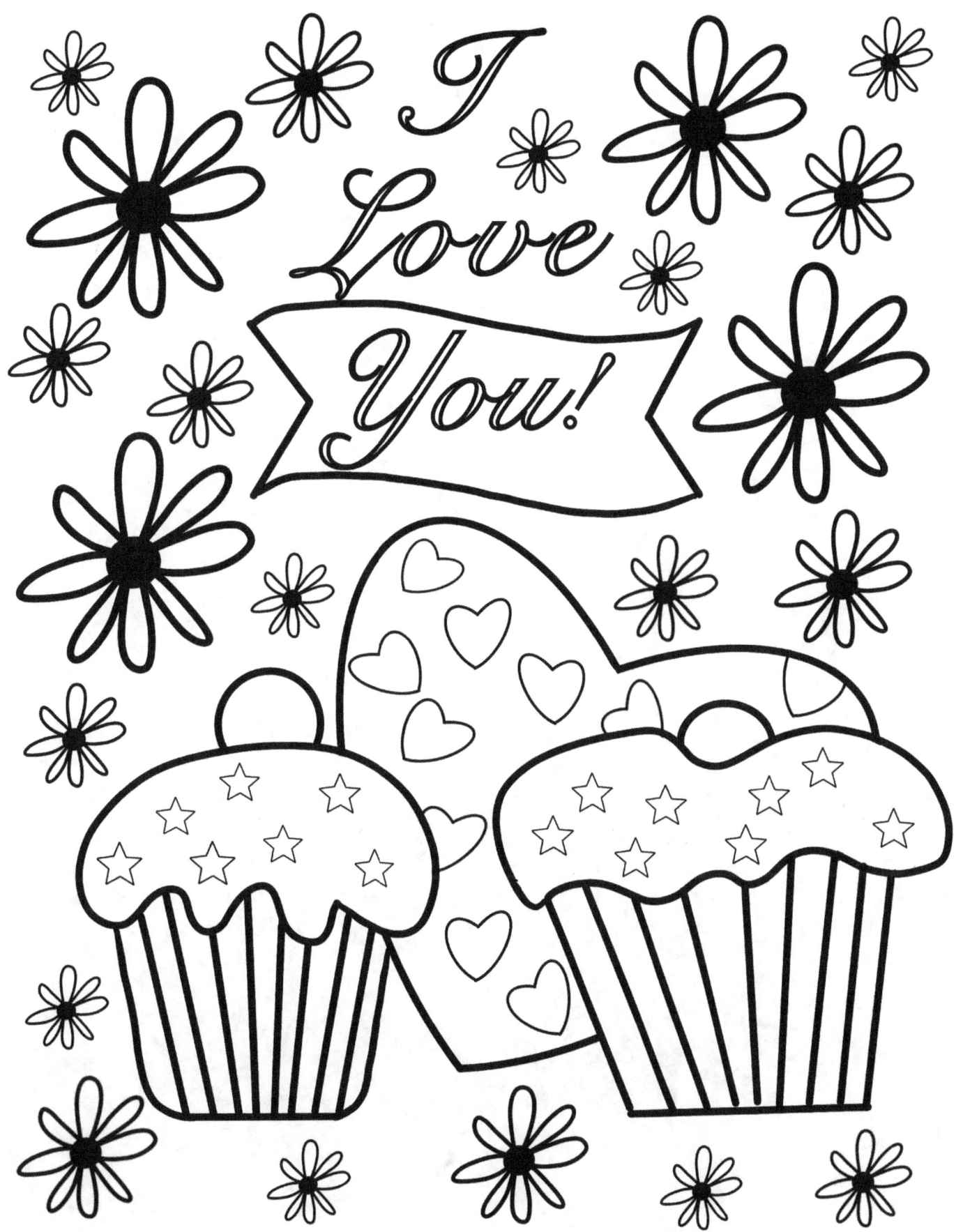

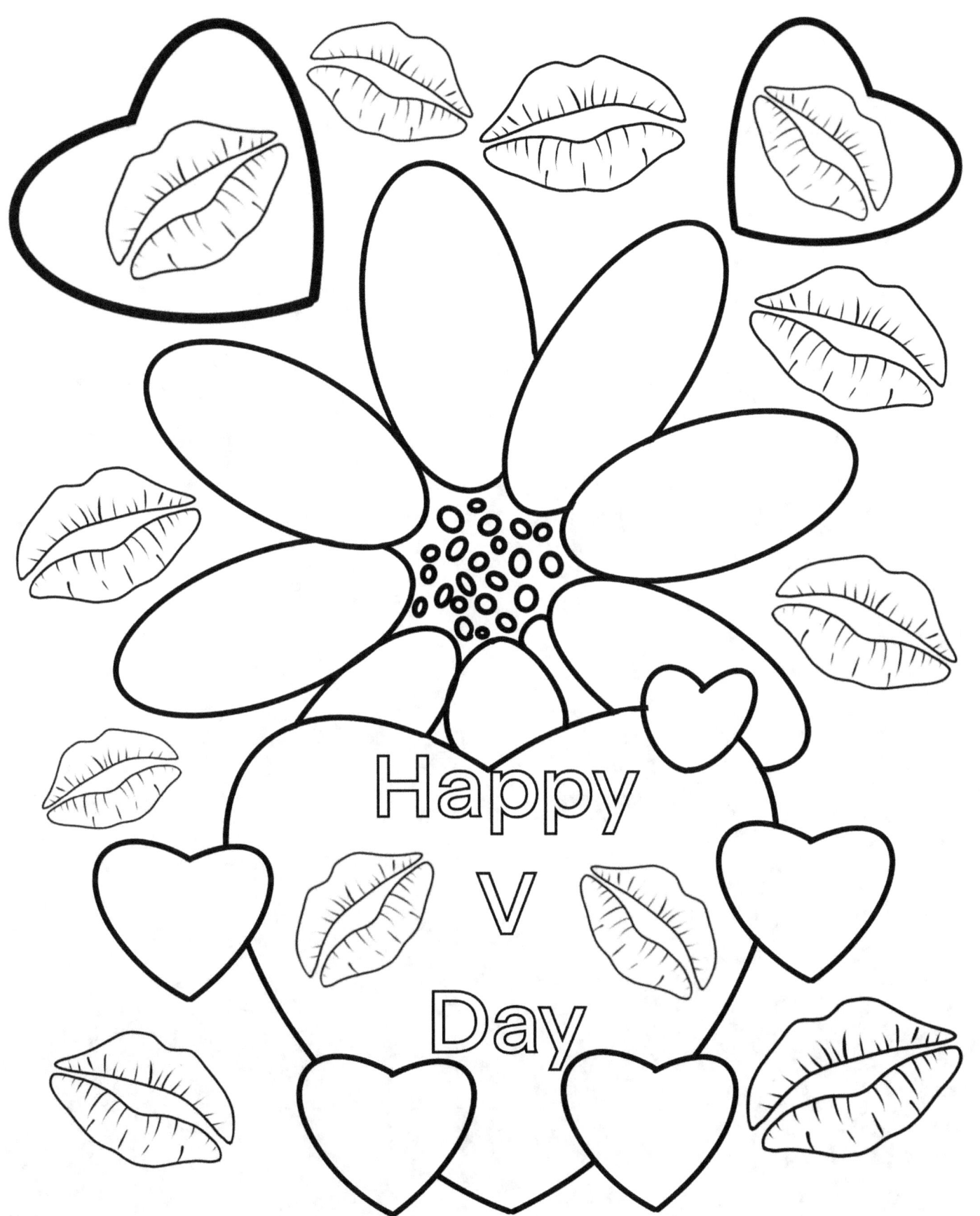

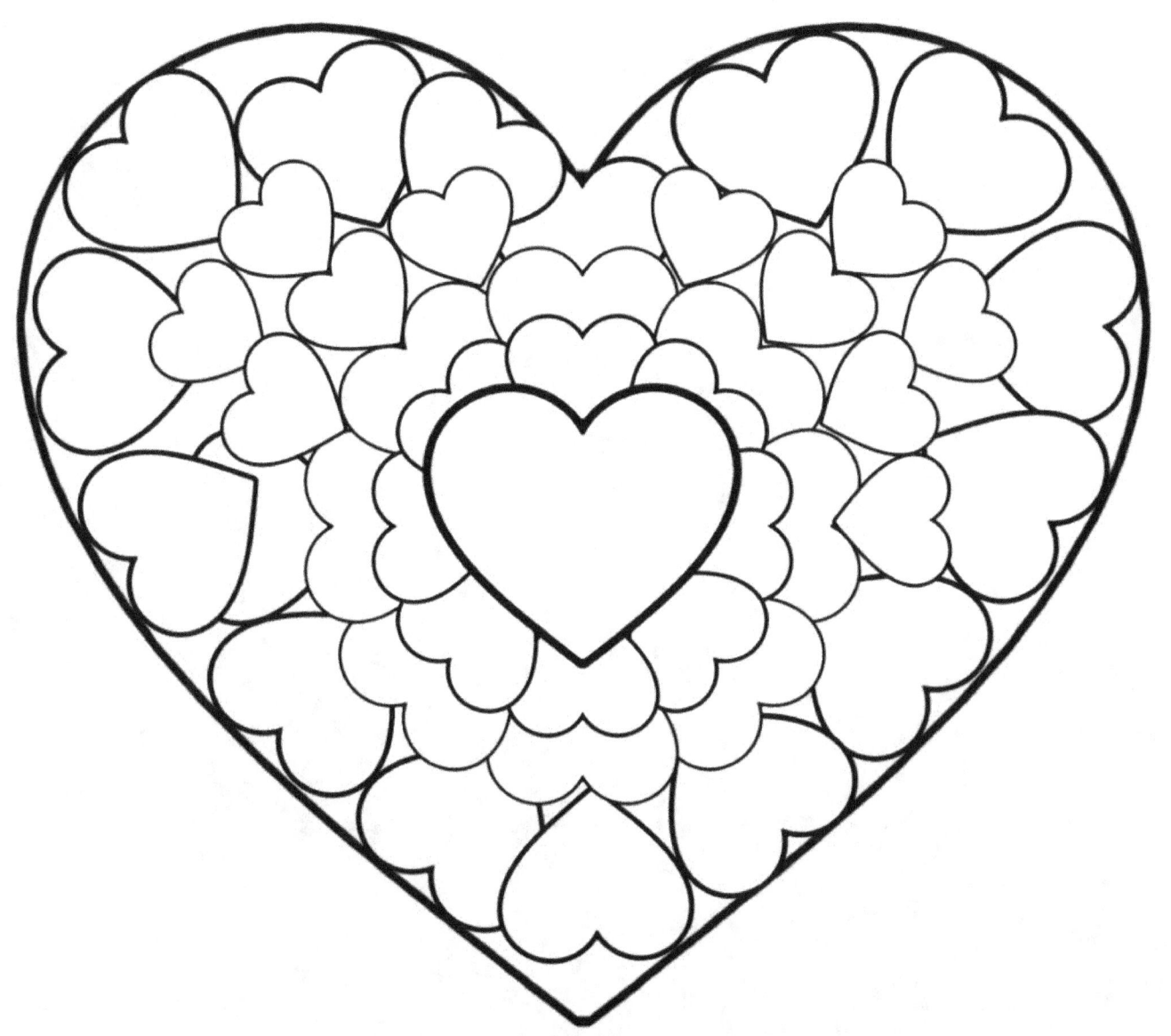

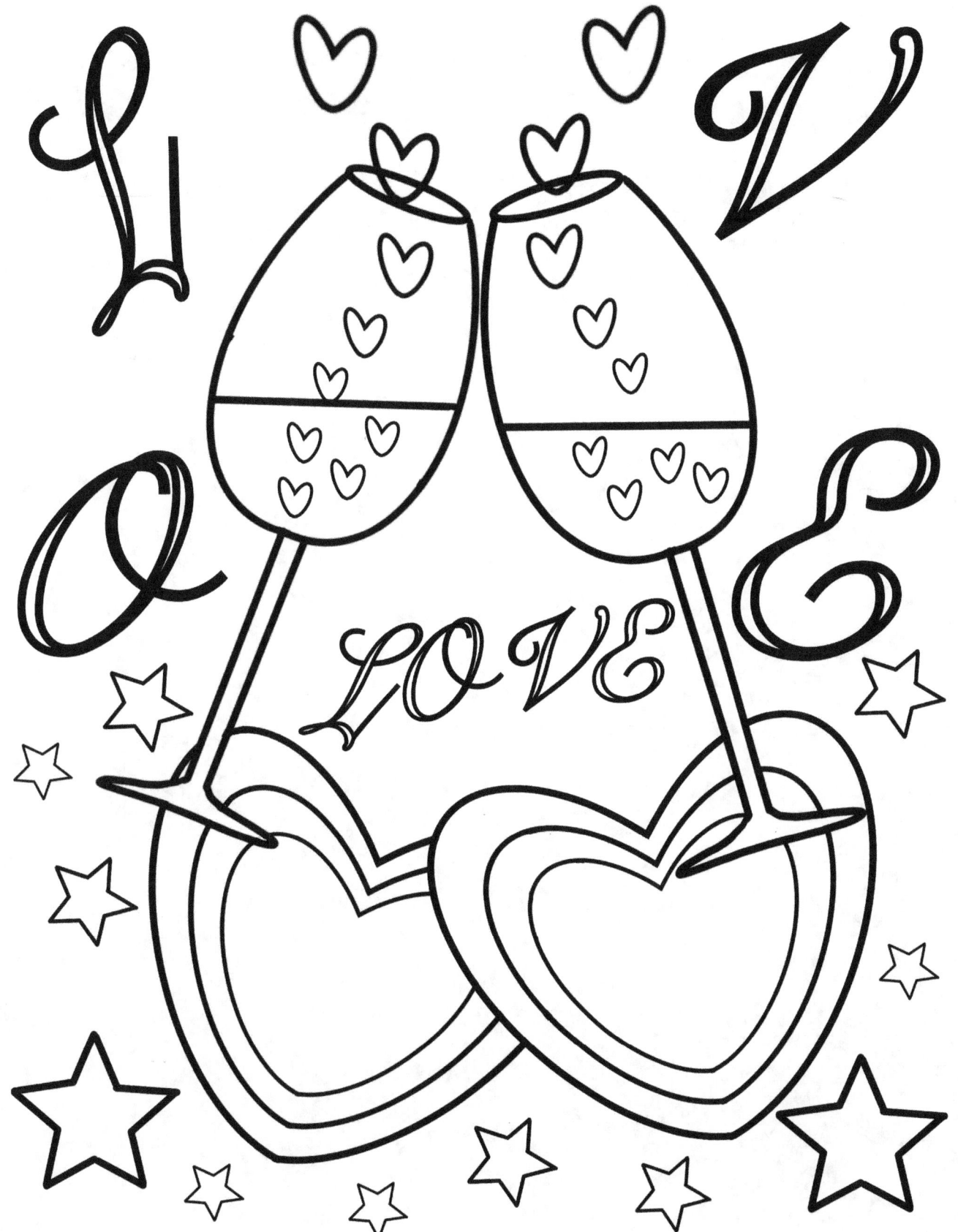

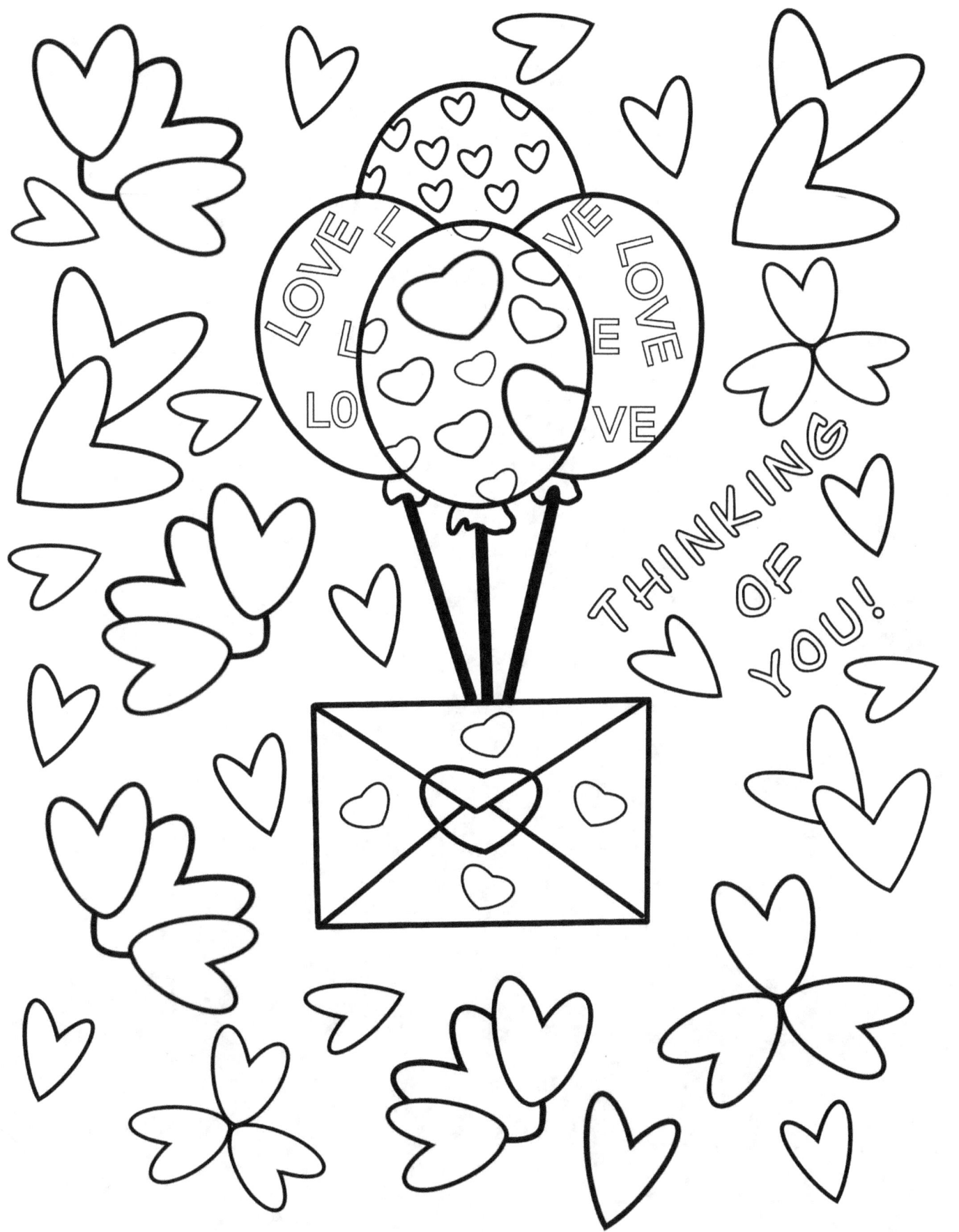

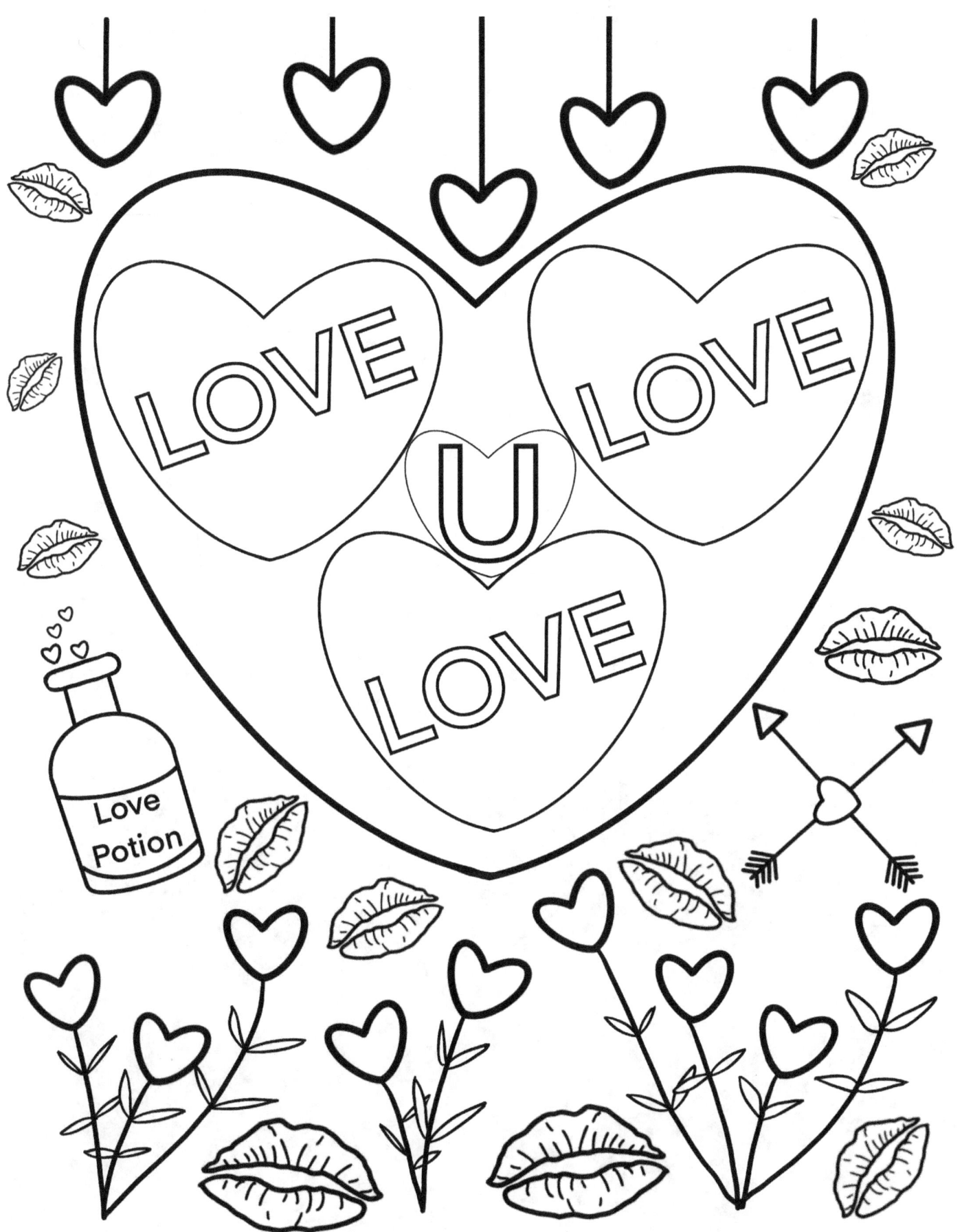

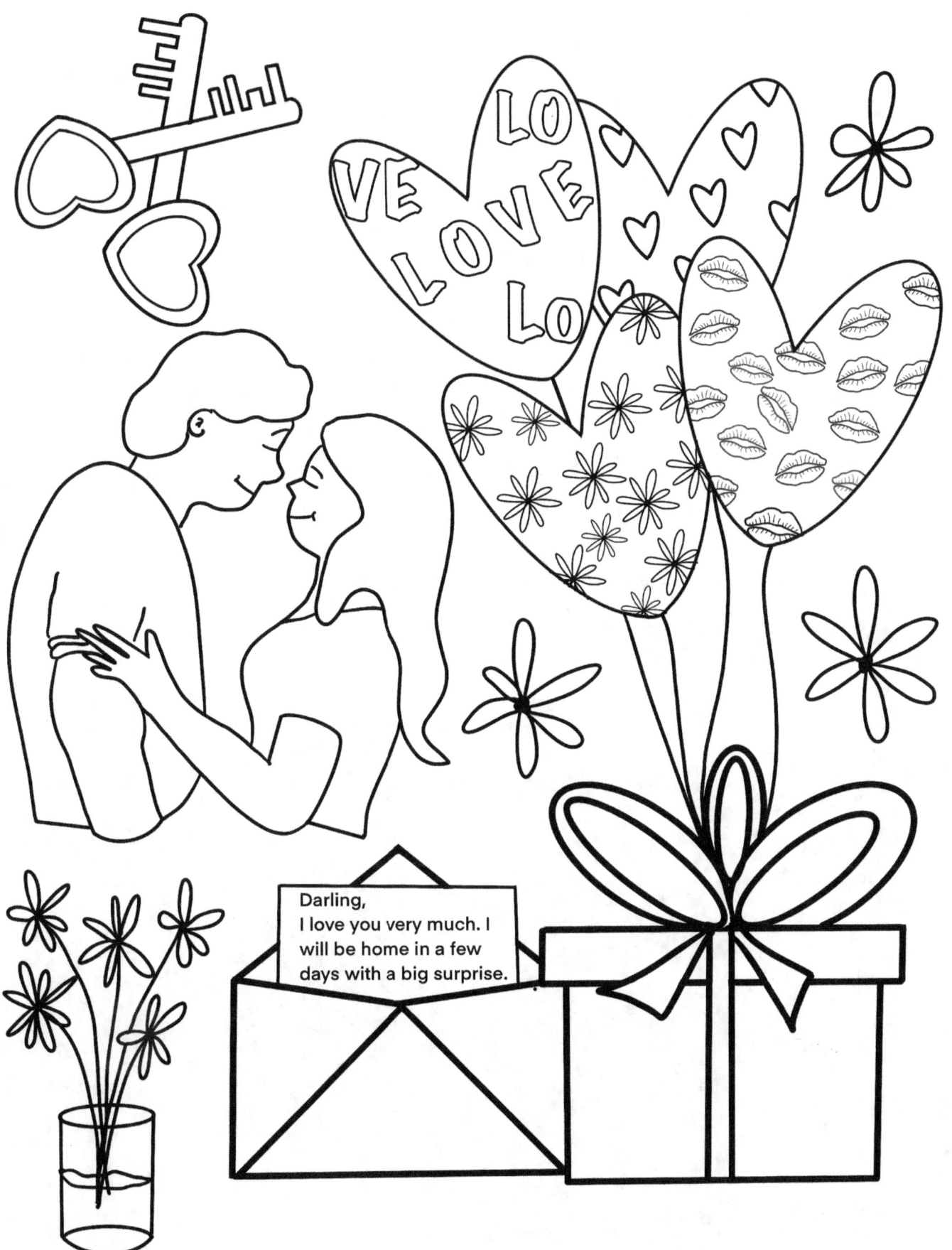

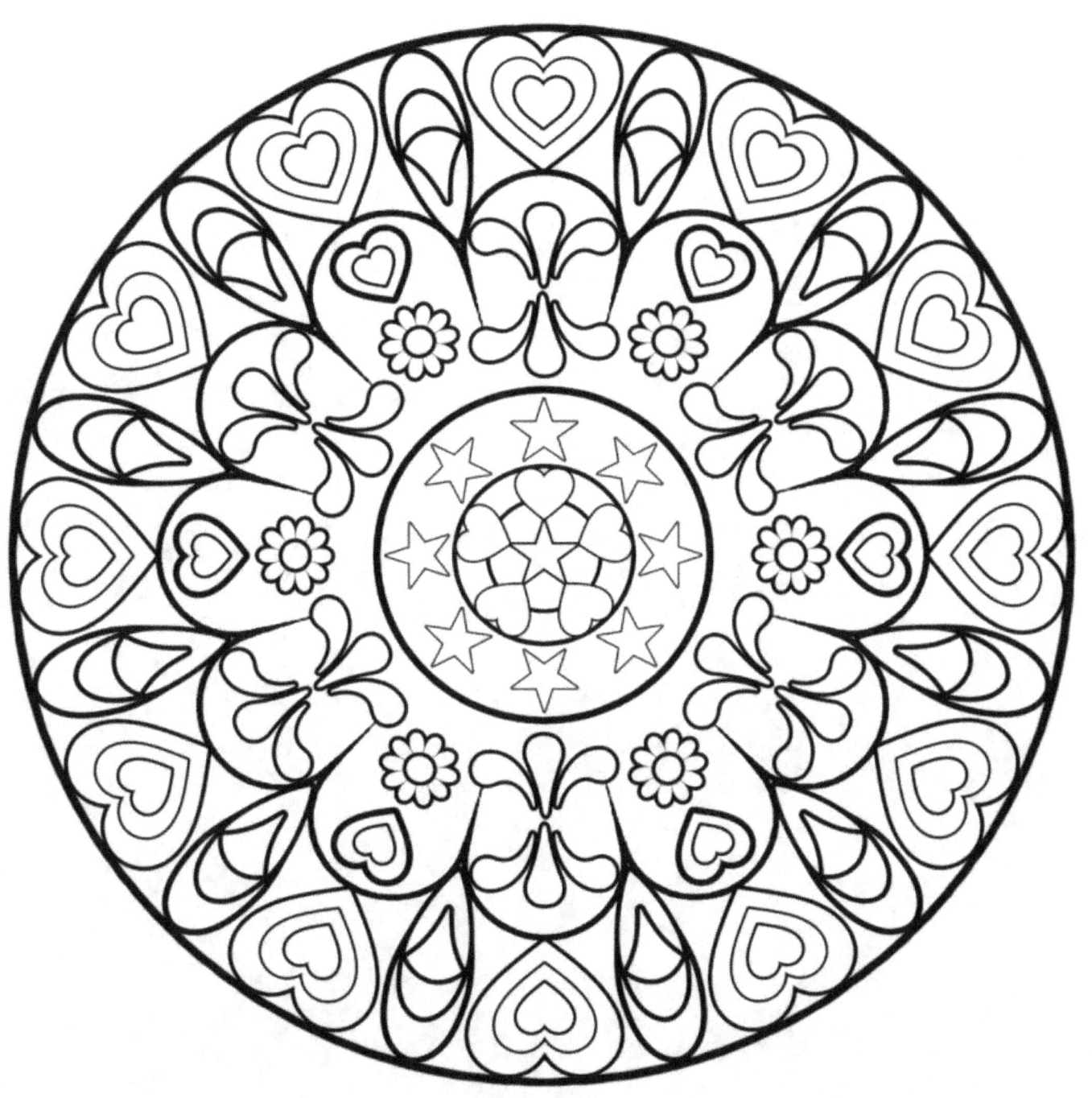

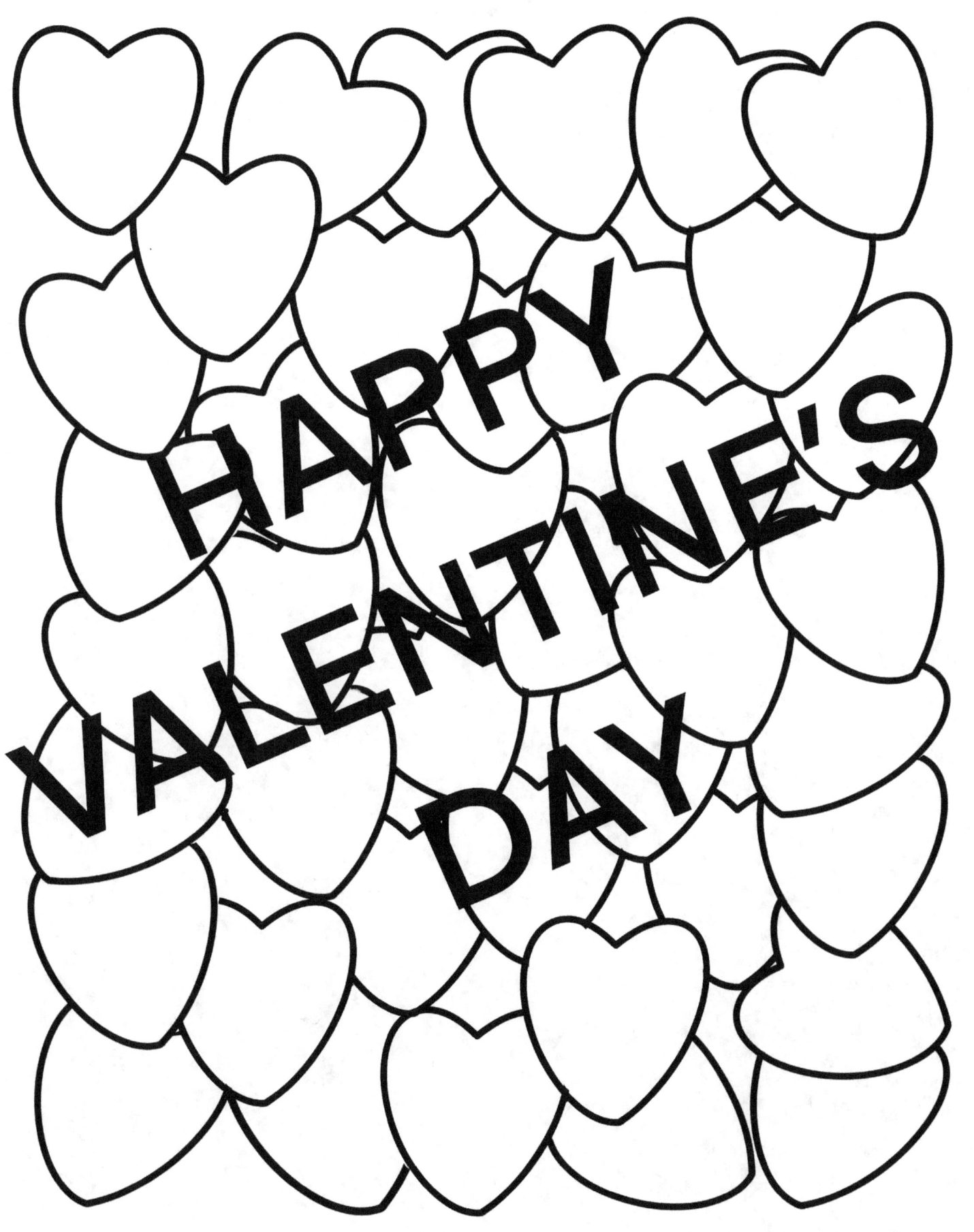

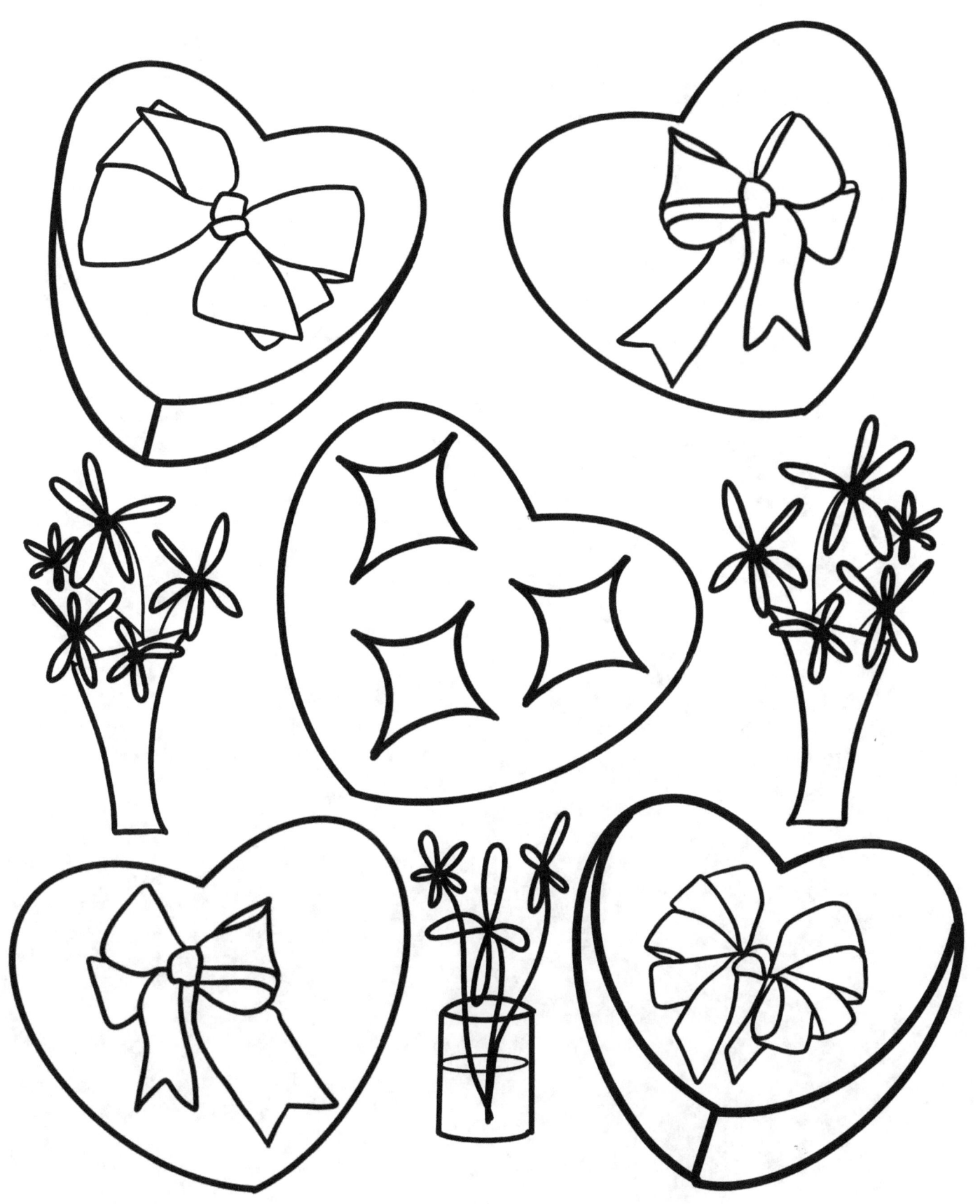

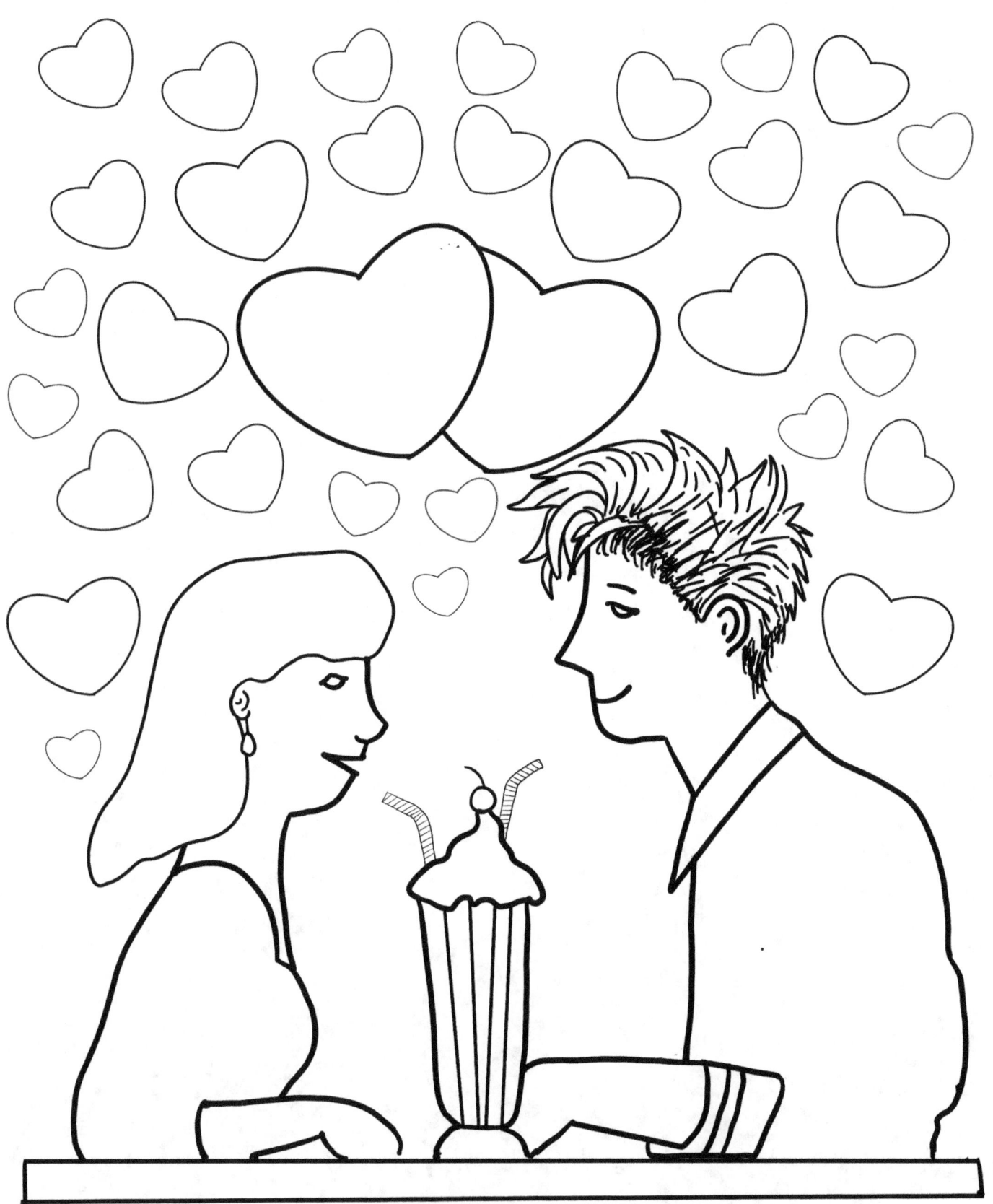

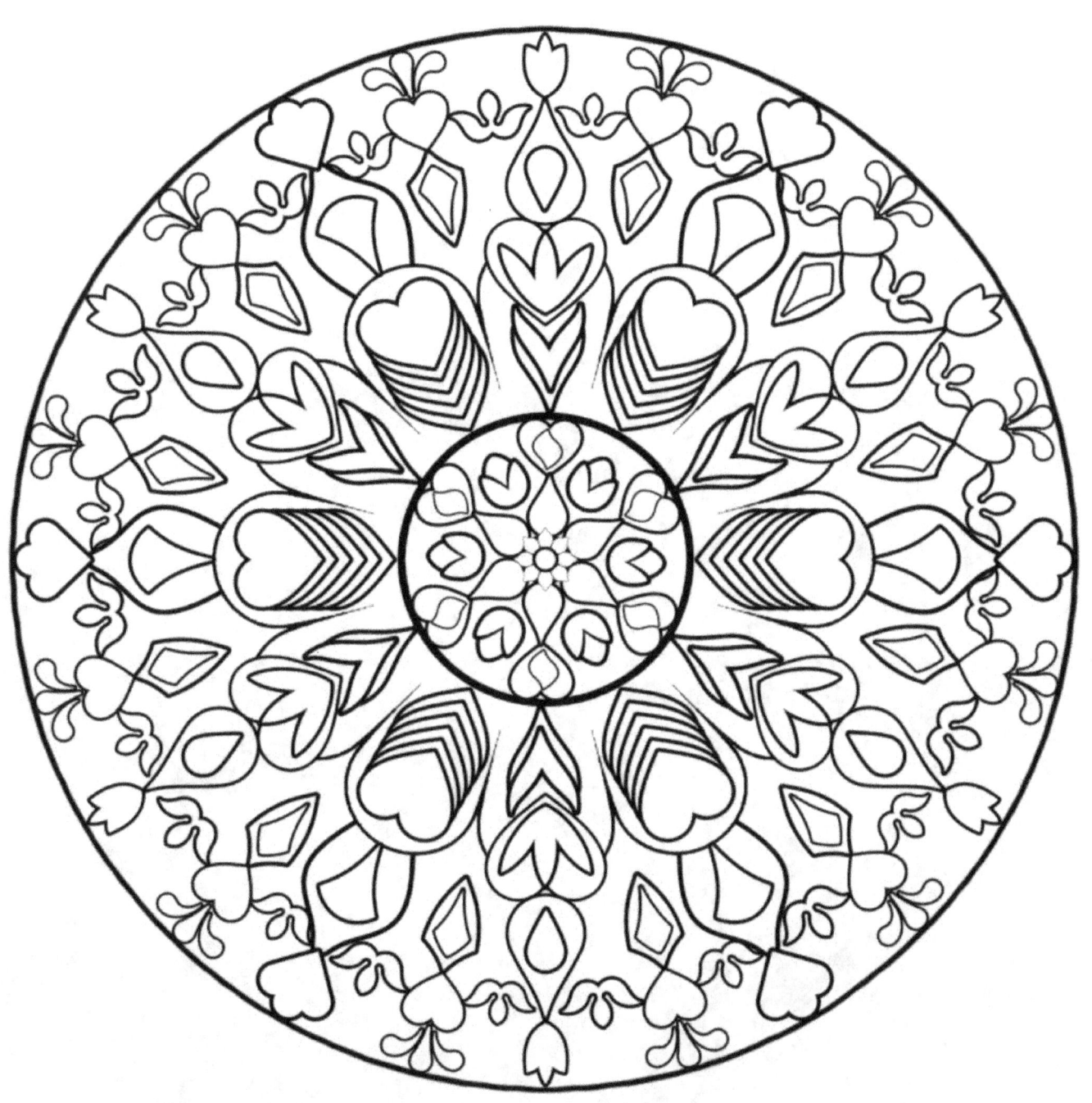

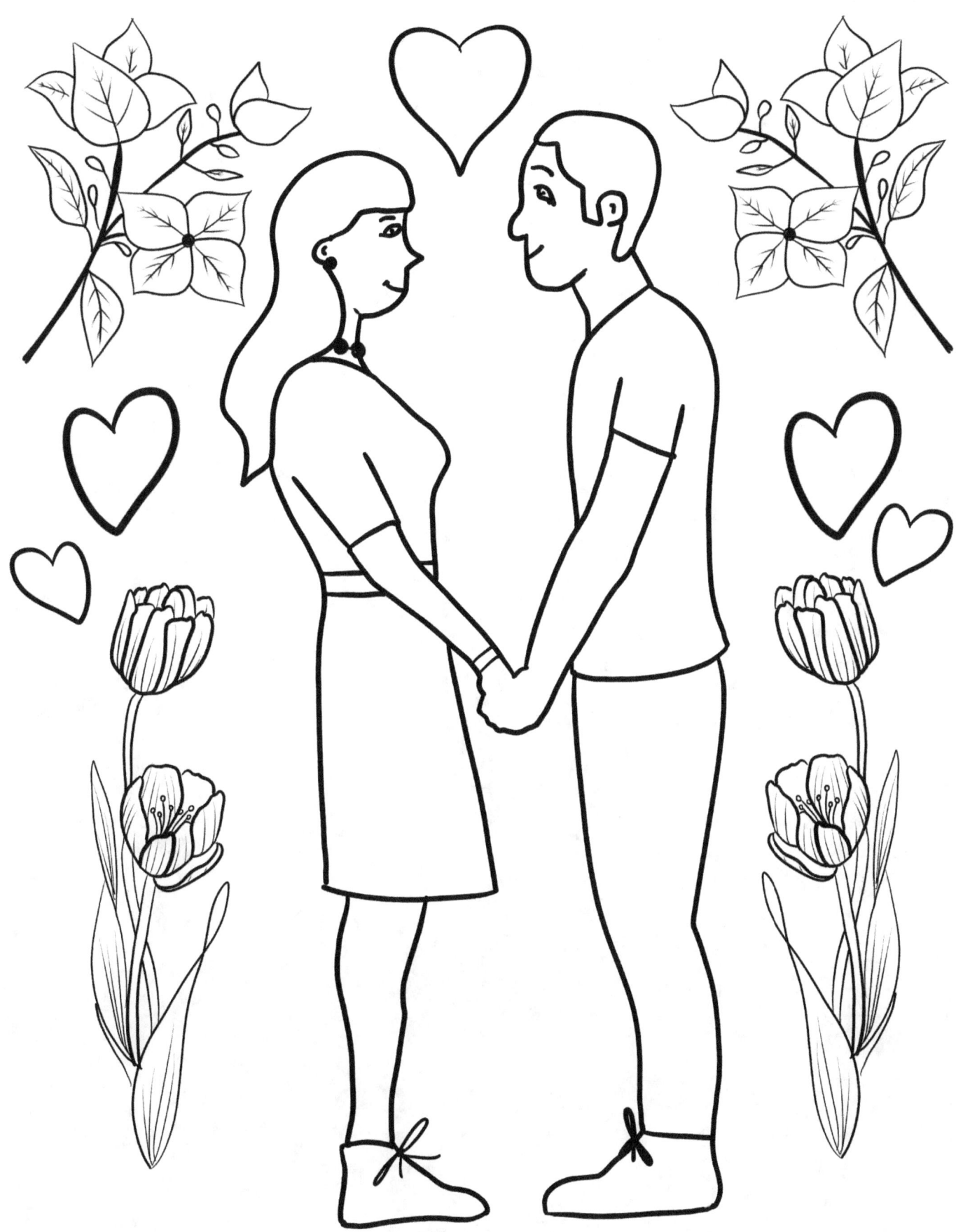

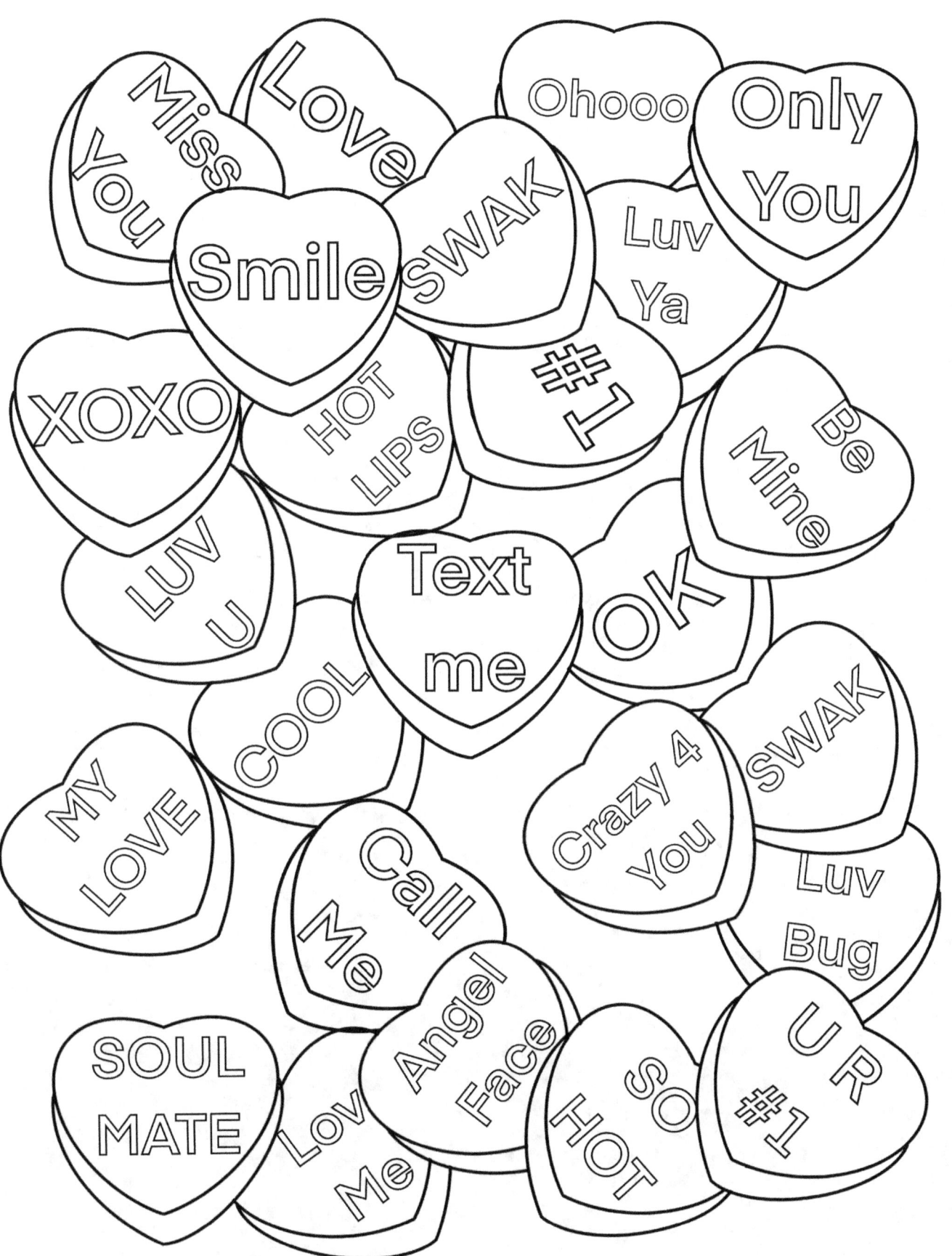

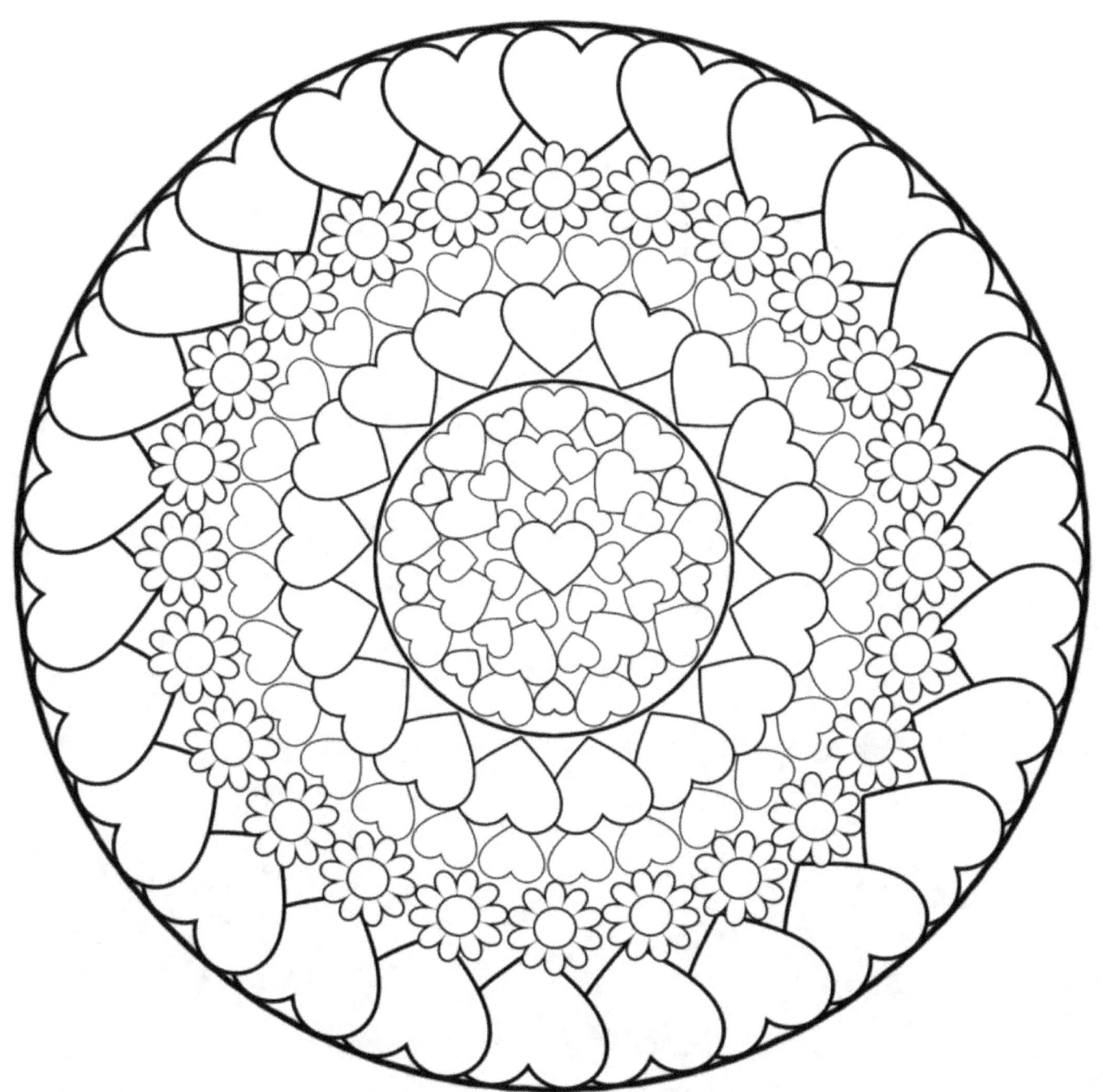

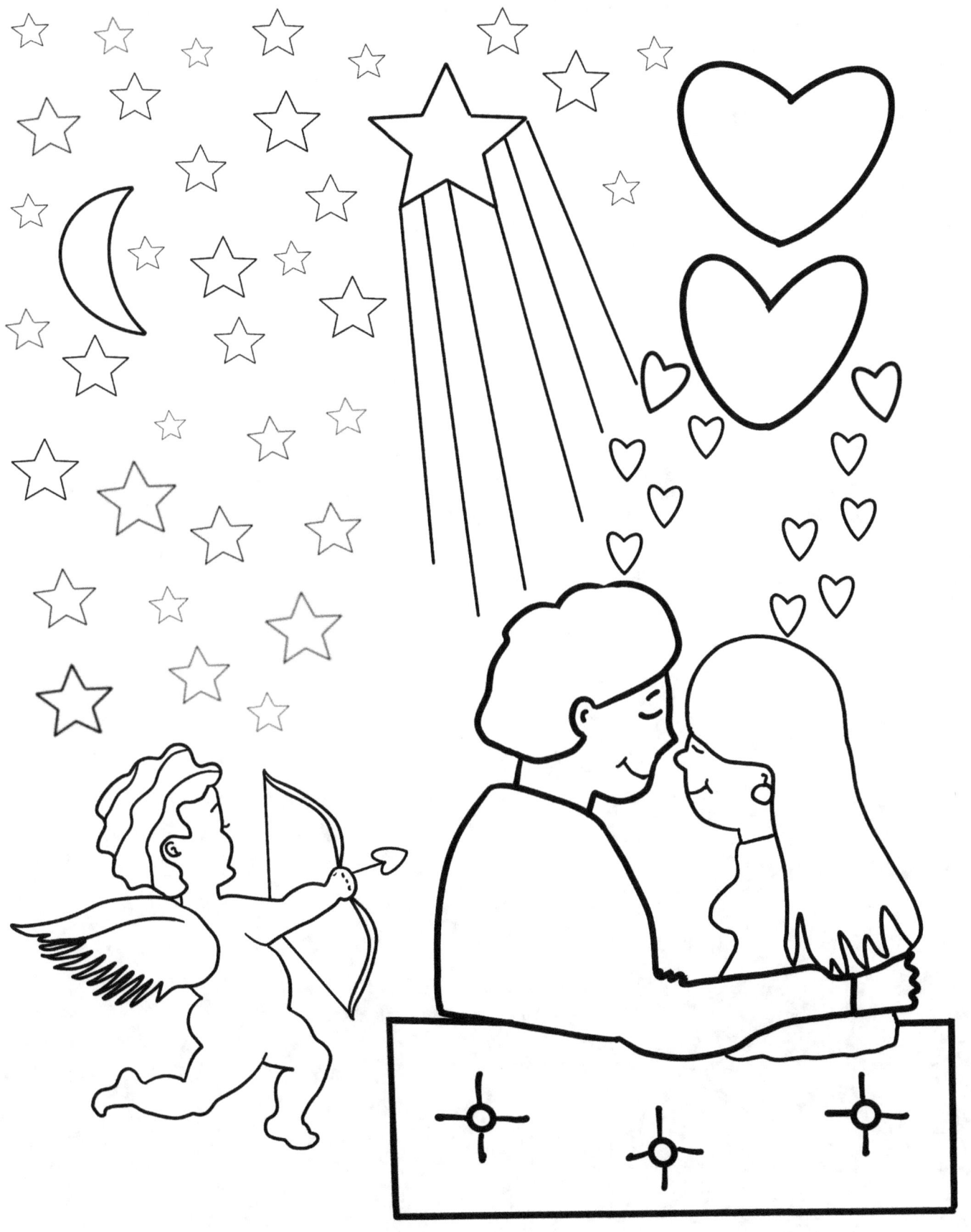

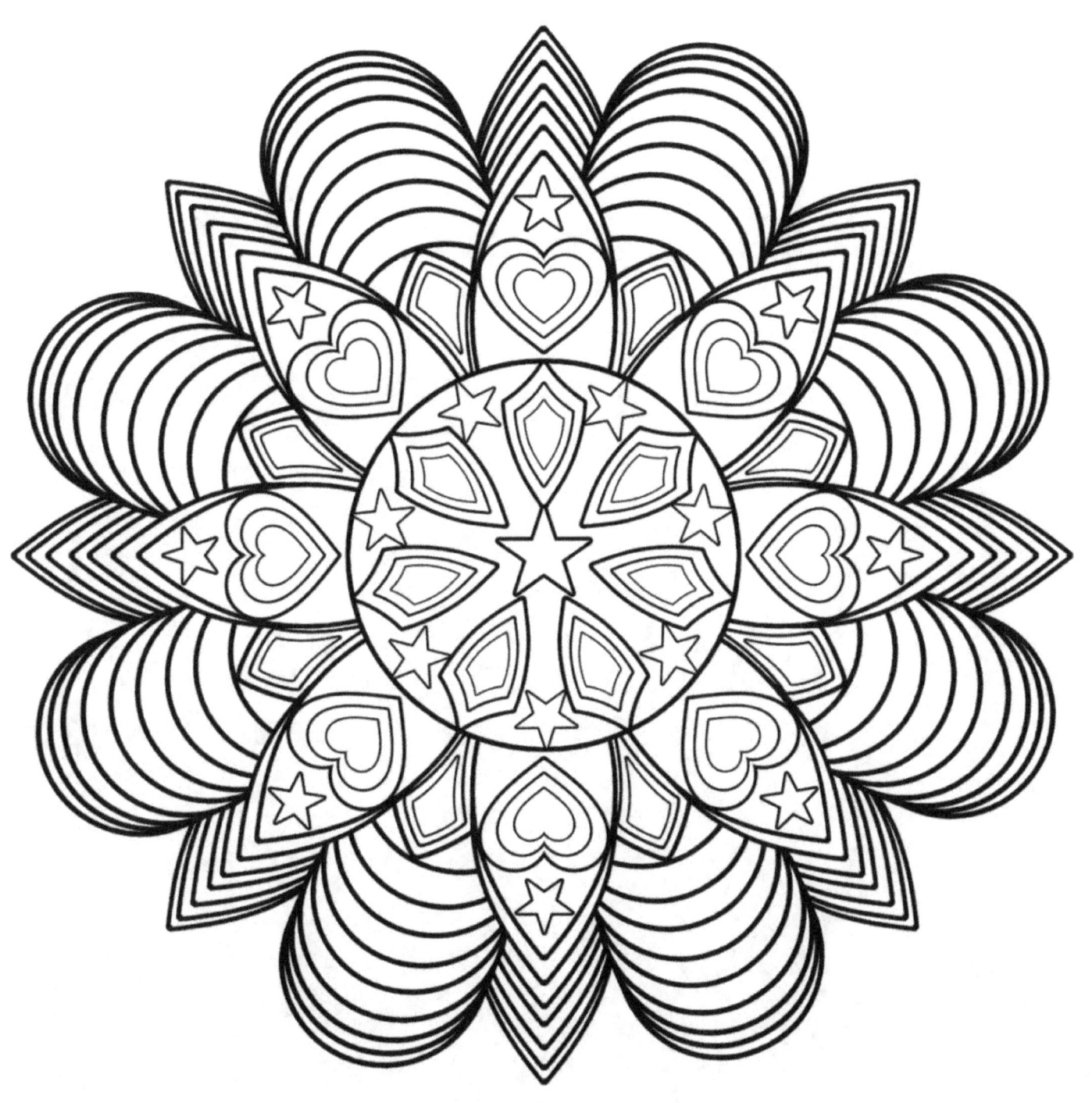

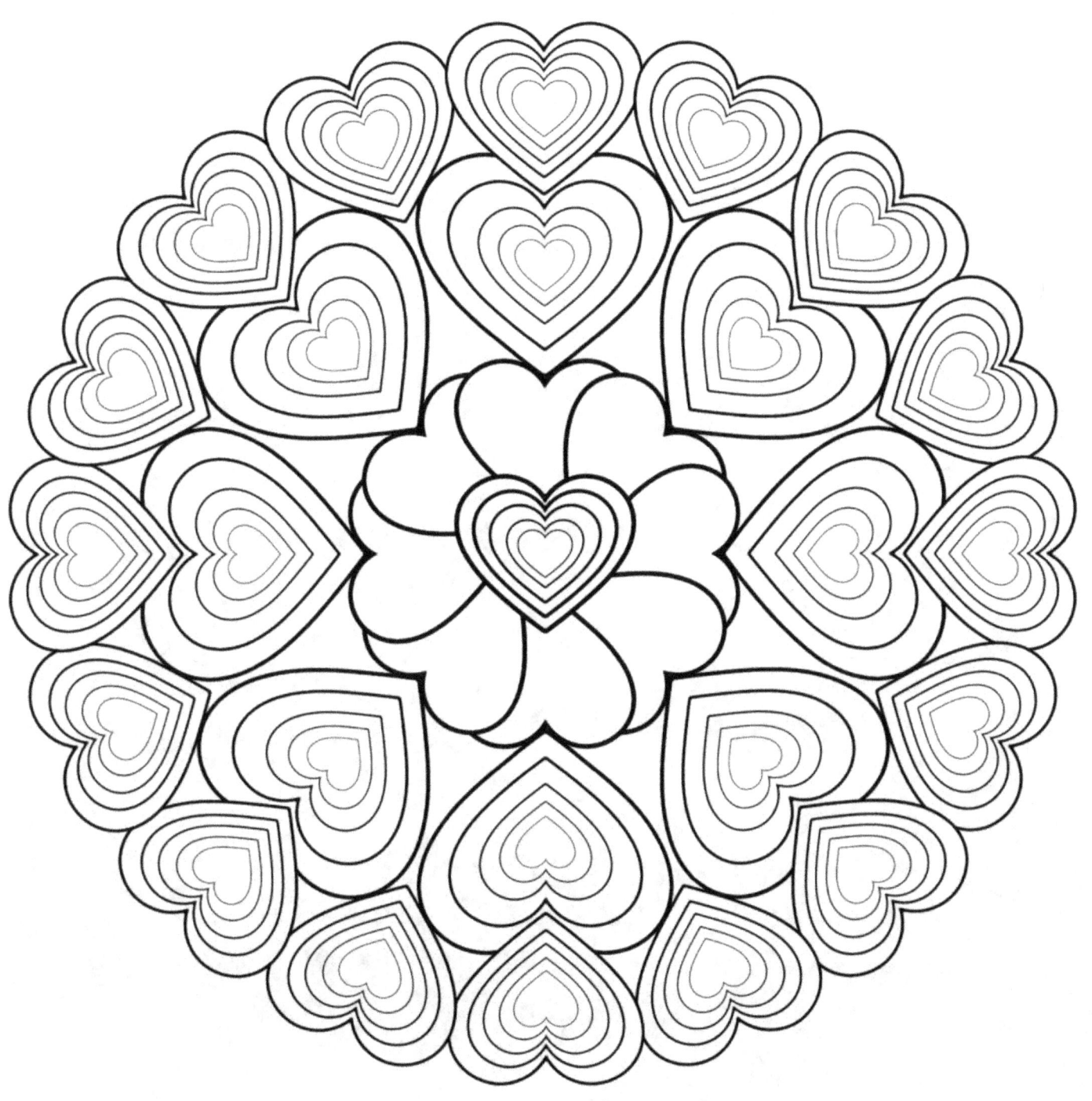

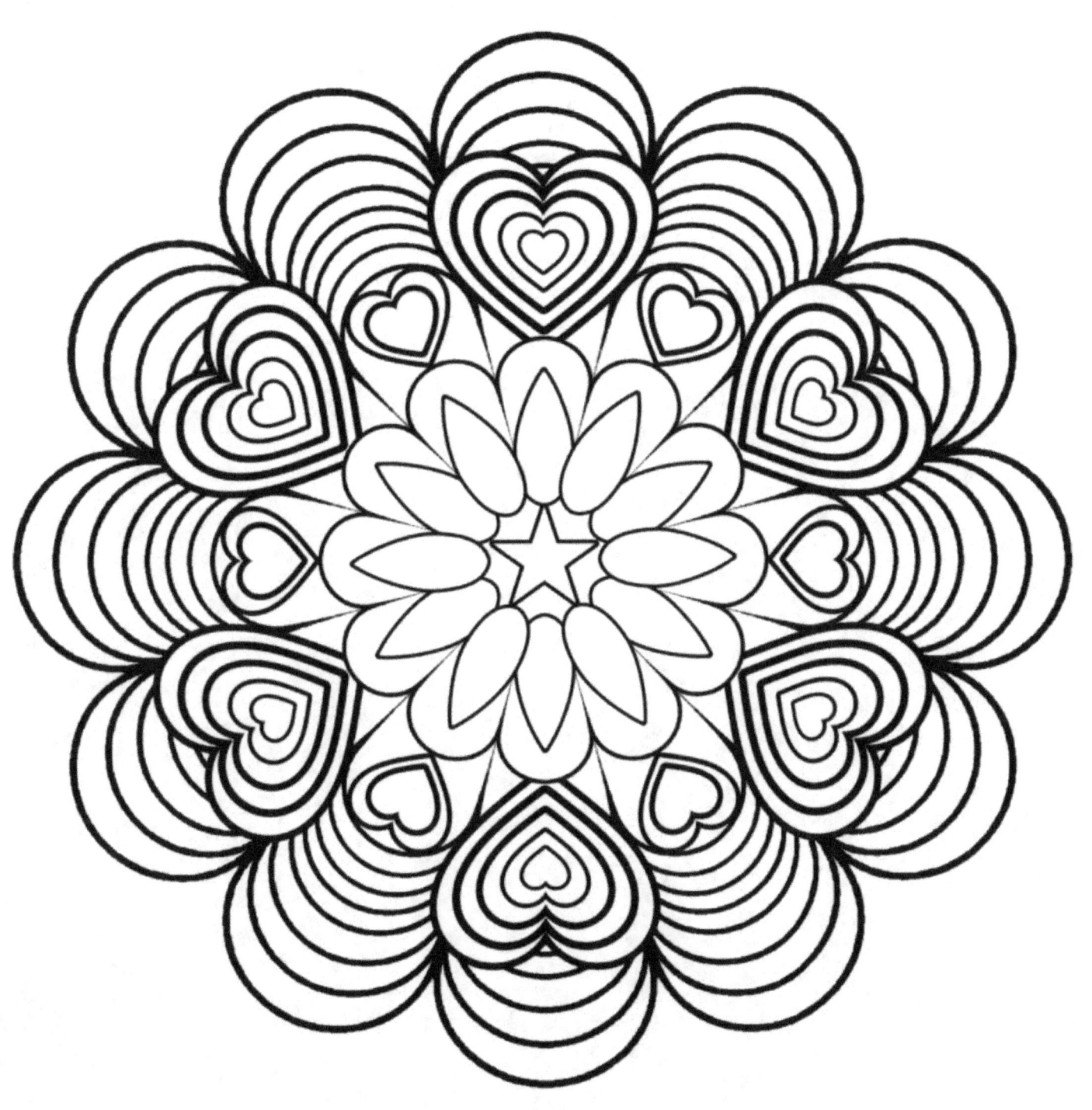

Thanks again for purchasing "Romance and Relaxation".

I hope it gave you hours and hours of fun and satisfaction.

I am currently in the process of designing and publishing more adult coloring books for you. Watch for them on Amazon and other bookstore outlets.

Wishing you all the best,

 Art King

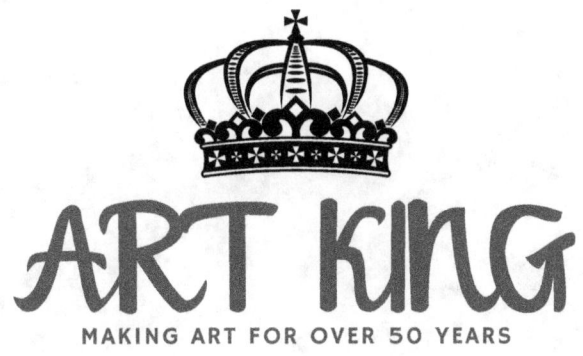

www.ingramcontent.com/pod-product-compliance
Lightning Source LLC
Chambersburg PA
CBHW080520220526

45465CB00006B/2548